JESUS & THE EMPOWERING INFLUENCE OF FRIENDSHIP

WHY GRACIOUS LIVING
IS MORE IMPORTANT THAN
RIGHT BELIEF

JOHN W. H. SMITH

COVENTRY
PRESS

Published in Australia by
Coventry Press
33 Scoresby Road
Bayswater VIC 3153

ISBN 9780648861256

Copyright © John W. H. Smith 2020

All rights reserved. Other than for the purposes and subject to the conditions prescribed under the *Copyright Act*, no part of this publication may be reproduced, stored in a retrieval system, or transmitted in any form or by any means, electronic, mechanical, photocopying, recording or otherwise, without the prior permission of the publisher.

Scripture quotations are from the *New Revised Standard Version Bible*, © 1989, Division of Christian Education of the National Council of the Churches of Christ in the United States of America. Used by permission. All rights reserved.

Catalogue-in-Publication entry is available from the National Library of Australia http://catologue.nla.gov.au

Cover design by Ian James – www.jgd.com.au
Text design by Coventry Press
Set in Tex Gyre Pagella 11.5 pt

Printed in Australia

Contents

Acknowledgments		3
We Are His Mates		5
Opening Gambit		7
Prayer by Michael Morwood		17
Chapter 1	The Significance of Friendship	21
Chapter 2	The Empowering Elements of Friendship	43
Chapter 3	The Way of the Historical Jesus	52
Chapter 4	The Values of Friendship	104
Chapter 5	Where Do Our Values Originate?	113
Chapter 6	Defining the Social Evils We are Experiencing	128
Chapter 7	Social Commentaries on the Current Circumstances	147

Chapter 8	The Role of Faith Communities	177
Chapter 9	Spirituality Without Borders	186
Chapter 10	'Our Role in Community as Subversives'	197
Chapter 11	The Future Structure of Inclusive Faith Communities	218
Chapter 12	Concluding Comments	237
Bibliography		247
Appendix A	Uluru Statement From The Heart	253
Appendix B	Common Dreams Statement 2019	256
Appendix C	The Words of Rev John Wesley in the Eighteenth Century	258

Acknowledgments

Most writers I have spoken with talk about the issue of personal and social isolation that occurs when one is writing. This is not only a problem for the writers, but also for those who are personally close to the writer. Receiving an inspirational insight can often lock the writer away for hours and even days to work through how this insight can be best expressed.

I wish to acknowledge my deep appreciation to my family and close friends who had to accept my ignoring of their needs during these times of isolation from engagement in important conversations. There have been times when my obsession with writing overtook my sensitivity to the needs of those close to me. To Robyn, my best friend and supportive partner, thank you for your love, toleration and support in the preparation of this book.

Finally, I am appreciative of the support and encouragement provided by my colleagues. I am indebted to many colleagues and in particular the Progressive Christian writers who have encouraged me to seek the answers to my questions about the value of living in community. Australian writers such as Rev. Rex Hunt, Rev. Dr Lorraine Parkinson, Rev. Dr John Bodycomb, Dr Val Webb and the Rev. John Gunson have been a wonderful encouragement to me.

I wish also to express my appreciation to Bruce Best for his advice and his professional assistance as a skilled proof reader and to Hugh McGinlay from Coventry Press for his advice and support.

I am also indebted to the writings of the social analyst and researcher Hugh Mackay in his compassionate examination of the current social problems we are facing in Australia today.

We Are His Mates

When Jesus rode in with his horse and his dog
And a couple of mates from outback,
We swatted the flies and sipped on our beers.
So why should we stir for this man and his God?

'Which trail leads to heaven?' An old drover quipped.
Said Jesus, 'Love God and your mates till the end.'
'And who is my mate?' the old drover yelled back.
'I'll tell you a story', said Jesus again.

'A bloke from the city came travelling outback.
When bushwackers hit him and left him half dead.
Along came a trooper and called to the bloke,
"Which way did they go? I'm hot on their tracks".

Then came a drover who yelled to his dog,
"We best keep away from this whole bleedin' mess".
But the black who came next brought the bloke to this pub.
Now who was a mate to the poor chap, my friends?'

John W. H. Smith

We followed this Bushman, this Jesus from God,
And we learned what it meant to be loyal and free.
For we are with Jesus and we are his mates
And we'll stick with our mate to the end.
 (Selected verses)

Pro Hart and Norman Habel, *A Bloke Called Jesus* (Rigby, 1982). Used by permission.

Opening Gambit

I am using the term Opening Gambit in place of 'preface', 'preamble' or 'introduction' because it can be defined as a 'phrase to initiate a conversation', or, in chess parlance, 'to initiate the game'. The primary aim of this book is to begin a conversation with my readers about the current status of values in western civilisation and Christian orthodoxy in contrast to the message and actions of Jesus of Nazareth. Further, I will explore how this Galilean sage was able to empower and transform the lives of those he met to such a degree that 2000 years down the track, people are still claiming to be his friend and are modelling their lives on his example. It is my firm belief that if Christianity does not personally engage with individuals in everyday life and if necessary challenge the wider community in which it is embedded, it will continue its rapid slide into irrelevancy.

After much deliberation and contemplation, I have decided again to put pen to paper. I do so in the fervent hope that this resulting conversation may encourage individuals and faith communities to examine closely the theology, policy, and practice of orthodox Christian tradition in the light of the message of the historical Jesus. The new research and enlightened spiritual awareness that is now available to us in this the twenty-first century, I believe, can open up a new and creative dialogue regarding the sacred source of energy we call GOD.

My initial deliberations have been ignited by the continuing decline of the influence of orthodox Christianity. This can be recognised by the rapidly increasing decline of membership in the established Christian denominations. This decline is primarily due to a general lack of regard for the so-called moral, ethical and traditional approach of Christian orthodoxy to the needs of our community and particularly to those who have been marginalised.

The lack of strong moral and ethical leadership has been reflected in the administrative church structure as well as in the proclamations of outdated doctrines and policies. This has been most clearly apparent in the findings of the *Royal Commission into Institutional Responses to Child Abuse* which were submitted to the Governor-General in December 2017 following a five-year enquiry. It is also apparent in the reaction of conservative elements of orthodox Christianity to the rights of same sex couples to be married under Australian law.

Loving relationships have taken a back seat to outdated doctrines and the protection of the church 'empire' has taken precedence over the rights of defenceless children. In particular, Christian orthodoxy has lost credibility, when its practices are morally incoherent with its stated doctrinal beliefs.

The orthodox Christian church has been more concerned about preserving the structure of an exclusive empire rather than promulgating the inclusive message and the sagely wisdom of Jesus of Nazareth. It appears that even the theological training colleges do not openly encourage students to challenge the orthodox tradition and they appear more concerned about defending outdated doctrines such as 'Original Sin ' or the 'Doctrine of Atonement' or 'Transubstantiation' than encouraging creative thought through an understanding of the metaphorical message of the sayings of Jesus of Nazareth.

The primary transforming medium of Jesus is his participation in personal relationships. If we wish to follow the path of the Galilean sage then we must modify our approach accordingly, by realising it is not so much what we believe, but how we engage with others that reveals the sacred spirit within that we call God. Jesus continually refers to the importance of treating each other with respect, because it is only through an engagement with the other in a deep personal relationship that we truly learn the values of empathy and compassion.

Rev. Dr John Bodycomb has pointed out that the leaders of Christian orthodoxy appear incapable of recognising the 'Elephants in the Room' – 'one is the future of organised religion in Western society; the other is the future of the religious professional'. It is clearly evident that modern Christian orthodoxy has an inability to accept the wisdom and experience of creative and scientific thinkers. Some critics have even suggested that there is a blanket denial by a number Christian leaders of scientific evidence, be it biblical scholarship, or science in general such as biology, ecology, sociology and global warming. Currently in this the twenty-first century, there are still prominent Christian church leaders, who do not accept that human activity has a significant impact on global warming. The evidence presented in chapter 6 shows very clearly that both western civilisation and orthodox Christianity are experiencing a moral crisis, due primarily to the values we currently prioritise. It is time to reclaim not only the message but also the morality of Jesus of Nazareth.

Perhaps one of the most significant reasons people find the church irrelevant is the language of 'God talk' that Christians use in public worship and published presentations, most of which make little intellectual sense to educated people of any age. Recently, while attending a church service, I was struck by the lack of logic that abounds in our church hymns and prayers, particularly regarding the doctrine of the atonement. I was plagued with the question, 'How would I explain to a teenager that 2000 years ago a person called Jesus died for their sins?' and then I asked myself, 'Why would I even try?'

What can we do about this? Well, I guess the first thing that needs to be done is to begin by proclaiming the 'message of Jesus' and not a 'message about Jesus'. I recently read a sermon presented to a Uniting Church congregation by a Uniting Church minister. The text for the day was Matthew's account of 'The Wise and Foolish Virgins'. In his presentation, the preacher mentions the inclusiveness of the kingdom of heaven as being like a banquet. While this is itself portraying a welcoming Jesus, the text also reported by both Luke (17:20-21) and Thomas (Saying 113) states that the kingdom or 'realm' of God is within us. If we believe this message of Jesus that the realm of God is in each person, then by sharing with each other we are bringing to visibility the sacred source of energy we call GOD.

The God of Jesus is the wisdom spirit within to lead authentic lives and to focus on sharing that spiritual wisdom with those people who are seeking something more in their lives. It is this that should give us cause to celebrate. God then becomes a verb and not a noun. This matter will be addressed in greater detail in a later chapter.

If all people have the source of spiritual energy within them, then 'gracious living becomes more important than right belief' and we must seek the source of spiritual power through our relationships. In a later chapter, it will be argued that it is Jesus' ability to see the sacred spiritual energy in others that made him a powerful influence in peoples' lives. It will further be proposed that our lives can be transformed through a spiritual relationship with Jesus and we have the ability to empower the lives of others through this same sacred energy.

My personal moral coherence is grounded in my belief that every human being is precious and demanding of respect, and as human beings we depend on one another to survive and grow. Consequently, we are responsible to and for one another, particularly to the people who are most disadvantaged. The wellbeing of community and society as a whole depends on the quality of respect, embodied in the interpersonal relationships between people, groups and the world in which we share.

Most New Testament scholars now recognise the 'voiceprint' of Jesus in the gospels and the newly translated sacred writings such as those found at Nag Hammadi. However, we still need to dig more deeply to understand how Jesus' words and actions made people feel about themselves and each other. The ability to evoke passion through relationships needs to be recognised as a powerful change agent in the activities of Jesus of Nazareth.

The message of Jesus is about how to live life graciously by sharing our experiences with each other and discovering through a form of Wisdom religion how to make this a better world for all people. It is a natural conclusion then to learn how best to do this within a safe community that is intentionally committed to the recognition of a spiritual energy. This book will explore the importance of Jesus' values in the way he shared his life with others. As Joe Bessler explains in *The Historical Jesus Goes to Church*, it is within a faith community that we can practise the relational skills we need to convey this Spirit of love and life, and by so doing learn how to recognise the realm of the God Spirit within. The practice of hospitality, respect, humility, disagreement and being community are all-possible in the activities of an embracing, inclusive spiritual community. Further, by practising the discipline of being a public body, people can grow through the embodying and enacting of the virtues of public life in a way that challenges and inspires others.

In the last twenty years and particularly in the last ten, I have witnessed a significant change in the attitude, life practice and beliefs of people who declared an allegiance to Christianity in its many forms. This change was most noticeable in adults, including people in post midlife, who had been struggling with the doctrines, worship and practice of orthodox Christianity. Their approach to living a wholesome life was now directed more to the pragmatism of living wholly and ethically within a community in a personal relationship with others. A majority of those who shared their concerns with me declared that religious faith could no longer withstand their intellectual integrity, which had developed primarily through life experience rather than from formal learning. In most situations this new learning came from close interpersonal relationships and the sharing of unconventional wisdom.

This new experience had opened up for many a universal experience, which led to the embracing of an energising consciousness about 'interconnectedness', 'inclusivity' and a sense of 'belonging' and wholeness not only to other humans but also to all life forms. It also raised for many a belief that it is their responsibility to ensure this message was communicated.

It is not just the young who are eager to learn, but people in their sixties and seventies who are keen to use their knowledge and experience to live fruitful and satisfying lives. Further, for many, their intuition has been challenged and awakened by the exploration of new scholarship provided by New Testament scholars. As a result, a new enquiring elder culture is emerging and encouraging people to embrace such matters as 'climate change', universality of humanity and the 'spirituality of the sacred earth'.

These people have outgrown the separation of secular and sacred. For them sacredness is universal, within and between all things and is to be found within our relationships with each other in the most pragmatic way. They embrace and promote intellectual development that is not necessarily associated with academic achievement. While they seek and promote both conventional and non-conventional wisdom, they tend to be dismissive of both secular and religious formal teaching. They seek wisdom through personal experience by seeking truth within a peer context through the informal exchange of knowledge gained from experience. What is interesting is that many of these people continue to maintain an association with an established Christian community. They may not profess Jesus as 'Lord and Saviour' but they recognise his values and ethics and they are committed to living their lives by practising an ethical and 'morally coherent' lifestyle that would challenge many religious practitioners.

Their commitment is to an orthopraxy of love, justice, compassion, and inclusivity and a more fair and equitable distribution of resources. Those from religious communities are realising that many people coming from different backgrounds such as left wing trade unionist and political climate change activists share these values. Clearly, many now realise that you do not need to be a member of a faith community to uphold the values associated with the historical Jesus of Nazareth.

It is interesting to note that many people in this group are critical of the formalised narrow approach to academic learning, in both public and religious academic institutions, even those who are graduates of this system. Clergy are confronted daily by people who question the value of these academic qualifications as opposed to the learning that arises from life experience. Diarmuid O'Murchu (2017) suggests we should envisage this section of the population as two interrelated groups, where he defines the first group as 'Wise Elders' who are seeking to explore with intellectual integrity a more expansive faith by engaging totally with the issues of everyday living. The second group is referred to as 'Seekers after a Natural Spirituality' who are those who are embracing a spirituality without borders and who are searching within themselves for ways of responding to an evolving and changing world?

This book will examine the elements of positive growth promoting relationships as propounded and practised by social scientists, primarily because, personal supportive human relations are by far the most significant change agent in society. This will be explored in the light of the current social evils that are pervading our society at this time and will include an analysis of the personal learning process of the 'bonding' and 'attachment' practice and particularly its influence on the values we hold.

In the light of these scientific findings, I will compare the life of Jesus, through his words, actions and values as recorded in the sacred writings, which will include not only the Bible, but the newly translated writings discovered at

Nag Hammadi some of which are recorded in Hal Taussig's edited book *A New New Testament*.

An examination of the structure and role of faith communities that profess commitment to modelling the life of Jesus in the process of empowering people through nurturing growth, promoting spiritually focused relationships, will also be analysed. I will then turn to the practice of orthodox Christianity to examine what, if anything, needs to be introduced or modified in its structure and practice, to effectively implement the empowering, inclusive message of Jesus the sage of Nazareth.

Prayer
by Michael Morwood

We gather today
mindful of the many times
we have professed our readiness
to be true disciples of Jesus
to be the salt of the earth
to be the light of the world.

We acknowledge the daunting challenge
of this profession
in the society in which we live,
with its economic systems
that impoverish and disempower people,
and its political systems
that enable the rich to get richer
and the earth to become poorer.

We remember that Jesus
encountered in his day
systems as unjust as those
we experience in our day,

and who surely felt powerless
to change anything on his own.

We turn our hearts and minds
to his message
to his hopes and dreams
to his ardent desire
for a better society.

We focus on his struggle
his reflections
his prayer
his questions –
where to start?
how to start?

what to say?
whom to choose?
how to keep going?
how to be salt?
how to be light?

We call to mind
how Jesus urged his listeners
to put their trust
in the power of being neighbour
in the power of God's Spirit within them
in the power of conversion
from religious thinking and practices
that made them feel inadequate
and worthless.

Prayer by Michael Morwood

Our prayer today
is a prayer of resolve
a prayer of determination
that we, each one of us,
will do whatever we can
however small
in whatever way
to bring the real dream of Jesus
to fruition
in our lives
and in our world today.

Michael Morwood, *Prayers for Progressive Christians* (Createspace, 2018), p. 147. Used by permission.

Chapter 1
The Significance of Friendship

It was drawn to my attention recently that there is a significant increase in the interest of personal ancestry searches and the desire to have a DNA test to determine one's ethnic origins. In my own extended Smith/Pocknee family, our eldest son and three of his cousins are exploring their family tree and their ethnicity.

From my discussions with them, it appears that there are many people today who are searching for a sense of belonging that is almost tribal, as well as a deeper understanding of their own inherited values and morals. It is interesting to note – as an older member of this Smith/Pocknee heritage – how often I am called upon by my nephews and nieces to recount my early childhood experiences, which occasionally go back two generations. The many photographs and letters that have come to light have allowed me to recall actual conversations with my mother and her maternal aunts.

My memory is such that I can recall quite vividly conversations I had with family members many years after the event. On reflection, I began to realise that much of my current behaviour was fashioned at an earlier stage of life by my extended family, and usually by people I held in high regard. My wife and Vickie, the wife of my nephew Alan, were remarking that Alan and I have an almost obsessive trait for cleaning shoes. Alan and I both recalled that my mother, Alan's grandmother and his mother (my sister), both experienced the impact of the Great Depression on the family income. Quality leather shoes were a major investment, hence the need to care daily for them. The financial circumstances that encouraged this behaviour have now changed, but we continue to regularly and almost obsessively clean our shoes, because the loving friendship we share with our mothers was such that we continue to honour their advice.

These searches into the family history have not only allowed us to better understand ourselves but they have provided us with connections with which to share this information. Many of these connections have allowed us to communicate through the social media network Facebook. These conversations have provided us with a wider circle of family identity, which has encouraged a sense of belonging to a clan.

These discussions have triggered for others childhood memories, which they feel have now been authenticated and reinforced by this cross-referencing. We have also discovered that friendships have been established and re-established, often providing affirmation for someone who is experiencing an emotional or spiritual vulnerability about their personal identity. Relationships are fundamental for our own personal sense of identity; because we are who we are through the friendships we form. Most people want to journey through life surrounded by friends that they can rely on. We celebrate and share our most intimate times as we journey with those who are closest to us. It is the informal personal networks that will influence the people we become much more so than the formal organisations be they religious, political or social.

We have discovered that friendship grows when we invite each other into a process of intimacy, which affirms our need for belonging, particularly for those of us who are suffering a sense of aloneness. Friendships invoke feelings; they also offer us the opportunity to experience empathy and it is empathy that encourages us to take on the passion of others. By forming a spiritual connection with others, we can experience their feelings and own them as ours. I contend that forming a spiritual relationship with Jesus of Nazareth we can experience the feelings that motivated him and own them as ours. Friendships have the greatest chance of success when they are built on shared values, morals and interests. People of all ages and stations in life seek friendships and consciously work to maintain their existing ones.

Relationships that value us as worthwhile human beings can bring us to a sense of wholeness. My mother had a significant growth removed from her back when I was about eleven years old. It was only after the operation that the doctors discovered she was diabetic. As a result, the large wound on her back took a long time to heal. It also meant that someone had to clean the wound regularly and because it was in the middle of her back my mother required personal assistance to do this. As we didn't have a shower, my mother would sit in the bath so that her back could be washed and cleaned.

On one occasion, I was the only person at home when this procedure needed to be done so my mother asked me if I would be kind enough to do this. I agreed so my mother called me when she was sitting in the bath. When I entered the bathroom, I noticed that my mother had discreetly covered her private parts with large flannels. She did this to preserve her own dignity and to help me deal with the embarrassment of seeing my mother naked as I washed and gently bathed her wound.

Our relationship took on a special meaning as a result of this experience, because my mother expressed her appreciation for my respect, care and gentleness and I became more aware of my mother's love for me by recognising that at my age I would suffer some embarrassment in seeing her naked in the bath. The established strong bond that was already between us grew even stronger and continued for the rest of her life because we both were able to respect and regard the feelings of each other. This experience also made me feel that I was capable even at this age to care for someone I loved.

Perhaps the question we need to ask is not, 'What did we understand about the experience of an embracing relationship?' but, 'How does this relationship make us feel and as a consequence how will it affect our behaviour?'

The Significance of Friendship

In an article in the *Sydney Morning Herald* in 2013, their senior writer Stephanie Wood raises real concerns about people who are suffering from loneliness. She reports on the life of a single man living in a public housing flat in inner city Sydney. Her interview is with Herbert Bowers who is asthmatic, diabetic and also suffers from a bi-polar disorder; and as a result of his condition, he is estranged from his family. In light of these discussions, Stephanie raises major concerns for the number of people who are suffering loneliness because of similar situations. She reports also on the fact that a number of social researchers have identified the condition of loneliness as a massive risk factor in ill health.

A well-known social analyst Hugh Mackay refers to the social problems of loneliness as R.S.I. or 'Reduced Social Interaction'. This condition includes not only social interaction but also the feeling of not being worthy enough to be touched.

I remember in my late teens living alone in a one bedroom flat in inner city Melbourne where I experienced not only the lack of social interaction, but also the importance of the lack of physical interaction with another person. In response to my needs for social and physical interaction I would, after work, catch a tram to Flinders St railway station on about four nights each week. Here, I would spend about 30 minutes going back and forth across the intersection in the busiest time between 5.30pm and 6.00pm. There would be a great crowd of people hurrying across the intersection between Flinders and Swanston St as people hurried to catch their train home.

As I crossed the road, I would be bumping into and touching other people and in some cases engaging in conversation. This activity made me feel less isolated and alone particularly because of the physical contact. It took me some months before I made contact with a group of friends who would take time to talk with me and at times embrace me when we met or went out for a meal together.

Loneliness is a temporary state in most cases, sometimes caused by moving to a new neighbourhood or when a relationship breakdown occurred. At this time, I was conscious of the fact that a number of males I met were experiencing a similar situation, more so than the females I encountered.

My loneliness reduced significantly when I enrolled in my university course and found friends who were interested in discussing the topics of the course and a desire to spend social time together. I became aware how important warm responsive friendships were on my personal development and the respect for myself because it made me feel I belonged and was well regarded by others. The importance of feeling a worthwhile human being was further enlarged when I met my future wife. Proving to me that my image as a person of value was contingent on the personal relationships I was able to form.

The Jews have a process they call 'Teshuva', which is about returning to the highest level of 'who we really are' after all the ways that we, as individuals and a society, have strayed in the past year. This includes each person considering what they have been doing all year long in their personal lives, work lives, and their relationships to

The Significance of Friendship

their family, spouse or partner, children, friends and to the larger society. It is a very deep and meaningful process that requires considerable contemplation and reflection and a preparedness to make changes to the way one relates to others. Michael Lerner, author of *The Left Hand of God* and the Rabbi at Beyt Tikkun synagogue, has facilitated a program called 'Teshuva buddy' where he encourages people to share this process with a friend, so they can check in each day to discuss whatever concerns they are experiencing as they work through this process. He recommends that the 'buddy' process should occur each day between Rosh Hashanah and Yom Kippur. Lerner believes that this buddy system of sharing will help each person confront the evils of racism, sexism, social class prejudices and other social concerns, in both the wider community and in ourselves.

The Teshuva process is a significant departure from a belief in theism, because it recognises that the evils of the world are the responsibility of each and every person and will only be corrected, through gracious living and caring relationships, and not through the intervention of a sacred being with human characteristics that resides 'elsewhere'.

Our daughter Emma works as a 'personal carer' in an aged care facility. This is not an easy profession to work in because it requires nursing skill and patience in providing for an elderly person's daily physical needs, such as toileting, bathing and feeding. It also requires a special sensitivity to the emotional needs of a person facing the reality of becoming old, alone and infirm as well as the frightening aspect of the unknown journey into death.

The task of carer is made even more onerous by the fact that the hourly rate of pay is one of the lowest in the field of human services direct care programs. Further to this, a recent study by 'Worksafe Victoria' revealed that up to 95% of health care workers have experienced verbal and physical assault from clients and family members. Emma's co-workers certainly need to be supported for the emotional stress that this work entails. After working her shift, Emma will often cook a batch of cakes to take to work the next day to share with other staff. When I asked her why she did this, she explained to me that the staff need to be a recognised and affirmed as special because of the work they do, and a few cakes cooked with love might help.

When our daughter arrives home from a shift, she sometimes needs to debrief by talking about her day, always in confidence. Each time she is attempting to put the experience of the shift into a positive perspective and to assess how she could have carried out her tasks in a more caring and humane way.

She always attempts to approach the people she works for with the dignity she would expect if she were ever in their situation. For example, she asks people when she enters their room if she can turn the light on and if they had a disturbed night and would they like to get up, or stay in bed a little longer. Though there is a routine to get everyone bathed dressed and ready for the day, recognition that the need for a little sleep-in is a personal matter is so very important. Economic rationalism doesn't necessarily work in human services especially if it works without the recognition of individual human need.

The Significance of Friendship

Emma sees her role as that of a friend, one who has time to listen. It is interesting to recognise that the word 'listen' is an anagram of 'silent'. To really listen requires patience and self-control to hold back from interrupting. She has grown attached to many of the people in her care. They may begin as patients, but in a short time they become friends. At times, she has gone back into work after her shift to sit with one of her friends who is facing the last hours of life. She will do this particularly if the person doesn't have family support. In one situation while sitting with a friend in the early hours of the morning, the woman's granddaughter arrived and sat on the other side of the bed and each held a hand of the elderly woman who was by now unconscious.

In the early hours of the morning, the woman died peacefully and the daughter said to Emma, 'In the last minutes I experienced another presence in the room, did you?' Emma replied, 'Yes. I often do feel another presence'. The girl asked, 'Who was it?' and Emma replied. 'I don't know. I just call them angels'. In that moment of the conversation, a bond was formed through the mutuality of their experience.

Human service organisations need to recognise that by encouraging personal care friendships they can ameliorate the sense of loneliness and fear that comes with dependency. Encouraging staff to recognise and respect the individual needs of the people they care for may at times disrupt routines but the greater benefit of feeling that 'you are loved' makes it worthwhile.

In working with people with disabilities the issue of acceptance and inclusion is crucial because, it is through the power of friends that many people with disabilities are accepted as valued members of society. A program such as 'Citizen Advocacy', which was developed by Professor Wolf Wolfensberger from the United States, provides support for people with disabilities who have been alienated by society because of their condition.

The cornerstone of a successful 'Citizen Advocacy' program depended on the quality of a one-to-one relationship with a competent citizen volunteer, who was free from built-in conflicts of interest such as those of employment regulations. The advocate took on the person's interests as if they were their own, in much the same way as a friend would.

Others have developed an extension of this approach such as John and Connie Lyle O'Brien, from the USA, and it was called 'A Circle of Friends'. Here, people known to the person with a disability were encouraged to provide ongoing friendship support in daily activities. The interesting outcome of this program was that a significant majority who were called upon to provide support willing accepted. As one person once said to me, 'As a neighbour, I always wanted to help the family but I felt I needed to be invited'.

In a significant piece of research conducted under the supervision of Professor Wolfensberger, it was discovered that those patients in a hospital who received immediate attention – when they pressed their emergency button – were people who had many visitors and an array of get well cards and flowers on their bedside table. Their calls were responded to almost immediately, whereas people who did not receive visitors or get-well wishes had to press the emergency button more than three times to receive attention.

An important aspect of these volunteer programs was that as 'friends' it is natural to offer companionship, support, assistance and a sense of belonging to the wider community. Whereas in many situations typical human services practices reinforce common prejudices and diminish severely disabled people's chances of making and keeping friends. In 2017, the O'Brien's developed a similar program for disabled refugees.

While studying under Professor Wolfensberger, I was accommodated in a L'Arche community in Syracuse New York. These communities were initiated by Jean Vanier and were designed to allow non-disabled people to share their life with people who had disabilities. Jean Vanier had been commissioned into the Royal Canadian Navy when he felt driven to do something more. He went on to study philosophy in France, and published works on Aristotle and briefly explored the possibility of joining the priesthood.

He found his true calling in 1963 after an encounter with two Frenchmen, Raphael and Philippe, who had intellectual disabilities. These young men showed Jean that they needed companionship and empathy and his heart was touched when he visited them in the institution. When Jean arrived home that night he realised how blessed he was to have the freedom to enjoy and explore his environment. As a result, he determined that he would share his life with these young men with the aim of offering them a sense of hospitality, friendship and belonging. Jean Vanier discovered that when these men came to share their lives with him, they were the educators because they opened his heart to realise that these young men, in return for this hospitality, could share love and a greater understanding of the depth of humanity. Vanier demonstrated that friendship and compassion for each other becomes a healing process.

I had the great privilege of meeting Jean when he visited Australia. He was conducting a workshop with a Catholic community in Adelaide when I was the CEO of the Barkuma Centre for people with intellectual disabilities. I contacted the community where Jean was staying and requested he speak with a number of C.E.O.s from organisations supporting people with disabilities. He warmly agreed to restructure his timetable and the group met with him for an hour. He was a most engaging communicator and held us enthralled as he encouraged us to see our role not as managers but as people who could enhance the healing power of friendship. As he was leaving the meeting to fly to Melbourne, he embraced me with a hug and to this day I still remember the warmth of his personality. Two hours later when I was back in my office, I received a phone call from him. He was in the Melbourne airport terminal and said he needed to ring me to say thanks for inviting him to share time with us.

Today, L'Arche has 154 communities and 21 community projects on five continents. Perhaps Vanier's greatest gift was to alert all humanity to an understanding that we all have needs and we are all incomplete human beings. However, by reaching out to offer support for those in need, we grow and become more aware of our own shortcomings.

During my time as the Chief Executive Officer of Barkuma Incorporated, I experienced many times the need

The Significance of Friendship

to be aware of my own shortcomings. One example remains strong in my memory. It occurred one morning on the factory floor while I was preparing the day's activities. I was suddenly alerted to a tap on my shoulder and as I turned around, Robert a young man took my face in his hands and staring into my eyes, he gently said, 'I said good morning, John Smith'. Robert was aware that I was deaf and instead of being annoyed that I hadn't responded to him, he was aware that it was my deafness that was the problem. Robert's concern for me showed me that I needed to be far more tolerant with others who were experiencing disabilities.

The importance of friendship cannot be underestimated in the wellbeing and respect of others. In Australia, we have a website known as 'Kitestring' which is dedicated to reducing the plight of loneliness by finding, keeping and maintaining close friends in a modern world. Their research discovered that: '1 in 4 adults have no one with whom to share difficult news'. On this website, they pose the important question, 'How can we structure our lives so that progress and connection aren't in conflict?' They set out very clearly that, although the world is expanding, the opening up of alternative opportunities to live and work often means that the time and structure necessary for forming close strong ties are usually missing.

This website sets out some strategies that may help people form and maintain nurturing personal relationships of quality. In a later chapter, we will examine some of the current cultural and political values from both social commentators and religious writers, including a number of Christian scholars who highlight the conflict between modern cultural trends with the moral teaching of sages such as Jesus of Nazareth through a movement called 'Reclaiming the Message of Jesus'.

These scholars have emphasised that the sacred spirit that the historical Jesus refers to as GOD comes to visibility not only in what he says and does but also in how he relates to others. The 'Moral Coherency' of the spirit of Jesus through his intimate experience of this sacred spiritual energy enables him to discern in his everyday activities and relationships the vital importance of 'Higher Order' values. For example, his 'egalitarian' approach to relationships comes from his firm understanding that in each person there is a spiritual energy of a sacred and divine source, which he refers to as the 'realm of God'. This is a message emphasised by the Jesus Seminar writers which has been adopted by people who call themselves 'Progressive Christians'.

So how has the movement of 'progressive Christianity' developed? In an article I produced in the book edited by Greg Jenks and Rex Hunt titled *Wisdom and Imagination*, I traced the development of this movement, which was primarily initiated by the scholars of the 'Jesus Seminar'.

The first task of the Jesus Seminar was to make an inventory and classify all the words attributed to Jesus from the first three centuries CE. Through an examination of the canonical gospels as well as independent sources, including those of Jewish historians, they collected more than 1,500 versions of approximately 500 sayings. In addition to the four canonical gospels, the Seminar included all other known non-canonical gospels in their deliberations, such as the findings at Nag Hammadi, which included a number of

'Sayings Gospels', one of them was the Coptic version of the Gospel of Thomas.

The scholars assumed that for a period of some years, stories about Jesus were circulated by word of mouth, and it is possible that more than ten years elapsed before anything was written down. It was another ten years before they were collated into the gospel form of Thomas. The members of the Seminar agreed to review each of these 1,500 statements, with the aim of determining which of them with a significant degree of probability, could be ascribed to Jesus,

The results of these deliberations are recorded in the 1993 Polebridge Publication *The Five Gospels – What Did Jesus Really Say. The Search for the Authentic Words of Jesus?* by Robert Funk, Roy Hoover and the Jesus Seminar members. Funk and the Jesus Seminar scholars followed up this publication with the *The Acts of Jesus. What Did Jesus Really Do?* released in 1998.

In the prologue to his book *The Historical Jesus*, John Dominic Crossan alerts us to the three major layers of the Jesus Tradition which are, first, the retention and recording of the essential core of words and deeds, events and happenings. Second is the development when applying such data to new situations, fresh problems and unforeseen circumstances; and a final one is of creation, which is not only composing new sayings and new stories but, above all, composing larger complexes that changed their contents by that very process. So to understand the message of Jesus, we must search back through these sedimented layers so that we can find what Jesus actually said and did.

It is this research and the collective collegiality of the Jesus Seminar scholars that provided the foundational material for the many valuable Resource books which were written in the late twentieth and early twenty-first century.

Why is it that these scholars and writers have had such a profound impact on our understanding of Christianity? Marcus Borg's book *Meeting Jesus Again for the First Time* captured for many the vision that grew from this research. People were indeed exploring the person of Jesus of Nazareth from a different perspective and for many it was a unique and fulfilling experience. But why did it resonate with so many lay people? Primarily it was because this approach raised for many the unresolved questions that had plagued them for many years.

The Jesus Seminar writers portrayed the historical Jesus as a revolutionary sage rather than a divine being; Jesus was presented as pointing to the saving power of God to transform and heal rather than to claim this ability for himself. This Jesus is egalitarian and inclusive in his table fellowship. He makes forgiveness reciprocal and he advocates that the relationship with God does not require a broker. The research also indicates that Jesus had to be set free from the confines of the creeds and doctrines, in particular the doctrine of atonement. Jesus' death as a blood sacrifice was in reality a later layer of information that had no basis in the findings of the Seminar. The research portrayed a radically different figure of Jesus to the one presented by orthodox Christianity. This in turn challenged our conventional understanding of God as portrayed by traditional Christianity.

These scholars paint a portrait of Jesus as an enlightened human being; a teacher of wisdom, which came from his intimacy with God. He was a healer whose powers came from his relationship with the divine and his understanding and experience of this reality. He displayed a compassion for the human misery and the exploitation of the marginalised that he observed. Further, he was aware that disempowerment was brought about through the abuse of social systems. David Galston, the Canadian theologian, writes that the significant detailed research of the Jesus Seminar, 'embraced the person – the historical Jesus and not a religious theme'. This approach affirms that history emerges out of a construct of what is said and done. The response to this scholarship did not lie within the context of the material only, but in how the material was presented. These scholars did not use academic language to convey their findings. Theology was not the sole domain of theologians but was being conveyed in a language that welcomed a wider audience. For many, these easily readable writings acknowledged and gave credence to the doubts and questions that many lay people had been wrestling with for many years. Some, in despair, had walked away from traditional Christian faith communities and had become – in Spong's terms – 'believers in exile'.

Writers such as Spong, Funk, B. B. Scott, Borg and Crossan were eagerly embraced because they offered people an understandable way of exploring a credible faith. Their writings encouraged people to meet Jesus again and to understand the context or 'matrix' of the first century life of a Galilean peasant. Crossan and Borg use the wisdom saying attributed to a Native American teacher, 'I do not know if this ever occurred but I do believe it to be profoundly true'. Which made so much sense to those who were searching for relevance and meaning in traditional Bible stories.

These scholars also encouraged people to 're-imagine a world' where God reigns by positioning themselves as eye witnesses to the events recorded in scripture. This was powerful and quite heady stuff for people who for the first time had been introduced to the practical application of New Testament scholarship in a language that made sense to their personal experience and knowledge. Those who were struggling with many of these issues welcomed the findings from these scholars and saw themselves as 'Progressive Christians'.

Progressive Christianity is a non-denominational approach to faith and spirituality that places an emphasis on how people live rather than on correct beliefs; and recognises in the person of Jesus there is a human life living in harmony with the Spirit of God. People who call themselves 'Progressive Christians' believe that the mission of Jesus was to demonstrate the power of love, to oppose injustice and oppression and proclaim that the realm of God is present in our world. So it is easy to understand why they embraced this new scholarship, which was supported also by current scientific knowledge and embraced intellectual integrity in affirming the individual's search for meaning. However, all of this information could only have impact if the mood of the audience is sufficiently in sync to resonate with it. On considering this matter, I became aware of an interesting parallel between the information being supplied to the general Christian community and the growth in the individual's spiritual development.

At a Progressive Christian Network of Victoria (PCNV) meeting in 2013, the Rev. Dr Chris Page suggested that people exploring their faith journey in the light of New Testament scholarship went through a series of stages. He referred to these stages as Enchantment, which is coming to an understanding of the person of Jesus as portrayed by the orthodox Christian faith. The stage of Disenchantment kicked in when this depiction of Jesus did not measure up to how they understood the world through their own 'knowledge' and 'experience'. The third stage that of Re-enchantment occurs when people discover a new way of relating to the Jesus of history through the detailed knowledge revealed by New Testament scholars such as the Jesus Seminar.

This new understanding allows us to live with doubt and uncertainty, which may often be the trigger that encourages us to begin deconstructing what we have become concerned about and in turn leads us to a delightful discovery of ourselves as mature adults capable of a personal relationship with the sacred, as O'Murchu suggests in his book 'Adult Faith' 2110. Hence it is through personal relationships that we begin to experience the humanity of the sage Jesus of Nazareth. The importance of supportive relationships in developing a healthy life can be seen in the work of the Kitestring website which is based on sound social scientific research. They quote the work of the Harvard Medical School's extensive study of Adult Development, which was a longitudinal study-taking place over a period of seventy-five years.

In 2015, the Director of this study, Robert Waldinger, said that, the clearest finding over this period was that: 'Good relationships keep us healthier and happier. Period.' Waldinger went on to record, 'That the best single predictor of people's mental and physical wellbeing at the age of eighty was the health of their friendships and partnerships when they were fifty'. It wasn't cholesterol levels or an exercise regime, it was personal connections through relationships.

In the deepest sense of the word, friendship refers to someone who recognises the possibilities in you that you do not see in yourself. It refers to someone who is capable of helping you realise your hidden potential. A friend is someone you can faithfully trust to share your deepest secrets. In a recent celebratory birthday speech for my nephew, his long time friend and work colleague Colin Murray said these quite profound words, 'Each of us possesses memory morsels of having been a part of your life and the music that resonates through it. It is difficult to explain the precise moment a friendship is forged. When a glass is filled, there is often the last drop that makes it overflow. In the meeting of eyes and a series of smiles and in sharing notions there is a unique something that makes the heart and mind overflow and at that moment a lasting connection is formed'.

Research by Kitestring indicates clearly that supportive relationships not only improve our health but there are indications that the benefits extend beyond our individual wellbeing to issues of social justice for all people. Connected, engaged and contented people are usually at the forefront of the movement for social justice. By talking and sharing together, we can find our united voice for the welfare of all people. With a stronger sense of belonging comes the sense of solidarity that gives strength to find the courage and wisdom to face the challenges of our time with courage and creativity. It is not about restructuring social systems or mission strategies; it is about nurturing interpersonal friendships.

It is friendships that invoke feelings because they also offer us the opportunity to experience empathy and empathy which encourages us to take on the passion of others. By forming a spiritual connection with others, we can experience their feelings and own them as ours. I contend that by forming a spiritual relationship with Jesus of Nazareth, we can experience the feelings that motivated him and own them as our own.

I have come to the conclusion and firmly believe that each intentional act of a caring friendship will be a building block towards a more connected and, most importantly, a more sensitive and compassionate world. Further, that the social evils we are currently experiencing in our society cannot be resolved through organisational systems because it takes an ethically based transformation through personal relationships.

A defining characteristic of the Jesus message regarding God's kingdom, as opposed to that of John the Baptiser, is what Anne Squire refers to as radical inclusion when she writes: 'The kingdom of God, as defined by Jesus, is a realm of radical inclusion, a society of radical equality'. All people are welcome in the kingdom announced by Jesus, including those marginalised by society or those whom Stephen Patterson refers to as the 'expendables'. These are the lepers, the sick, disabled, prostitutes and tax collectors.

Squire concludes that with the church today in decline and mired in outdated beliefs and practice, we need to reclaim the kingdom way of Jesus of Nazareth, where all are included, welcomed and embraced. By so doing, we will live the dream of the sage of Nazareth.

The recognition that people excluded by mainstream society are included in God's kingdom is countercultural. Hospitality and inclusion take precedence over the purity laws, as we witness in the story of the woman who had been haemorrhaging for twelve years (Matthew 9:20-22). We read that Jesus and his disciples eat with defiled hands i.e. they do not wash before eating and Jesus allows people considered unclean to touch him (Mark 1:41 and Luke 7:36-50).

The instructions given to the seventy disciples when they set out on their missionary task are to eat and drink what has been prepared by those who are providing the hospitality (Luke 10:7). Jesus is saying to his disciples that affirmation of inclusion and gratitude for being included is far more important than purity laws.

Chapter 2

The Empowering Elements of Friendship

How do people cope with personal issues when living in a world that is fraught with the divisive matters? I would argue that the majority of people in our society survive and grow, even in the most dire circumstances, when they have mutually supportive personal relationships. I am referring to those personal relationships that provide the emotional support necessary to cope with the day-to-day pressures of modern living.

Through their daily relationships, the majority of Australia's population have experience of people struggling with issues of domestic violence toward women. We meet others who are trying, in difficult financial times, to make ends meet in a world of low wages, rising prices and economic inequality. Then there are those who have become victims of hostility and abuse simply as a result of their gender, ethnic origin, skin colour, religious belief or sexual orientation.

How can we as individuals assist those who have been disadvantaged by prejudiced social attitudes and economic conditions that continue to isolate and reject them? I firmly believe that it is the 'transforming power of friendship' that will provide people with the emotional energy they require to meet the challenges of these social evils.

In its most meaningful interpretation, the word 'friend' is defined as someone who recognises in you a greater potential than you have imagined for yourself. It is someone who can enable and empower you to become the person you are capable of being. It takes only one person through friendship to stand in solidarity with another to be a 'transforming' influence.

How then do positive, long term and mutually supportive relationships develop and what are the elements of a good relationship? Or, perhaps more importantly, how can we, in our daily lives, make a contribution to the wellbeing of the community so as to diminish the damage created by the social evils that confront us on a daily basis?

Most psychologists and social scientists support the understanding that there are certain elements in the establishment of a friendship that will encourage a mutually positive, growth-promoting relation with people we meet. It is through personal relationships that we find the resources not only to protect ourselves from the impact of these social evils but also to ensure that these evils have a minimal impact on those with whom we engage. How then can we assist others to find a meaningful, enriching, exciting, rewarding and challenging life?

The Empowering Elements of Friendship

The social research shows that a good life occurs when an individual realises that they have been deeply heard because they truly believe that they are understood and accepted for who they are. Friendships can provide direction, but not necessarily destination.

The change that occurs through friendship will affect all involved. To share your life with someone in this way will sometimes mean that you will need to lay aside your own views and values in order to enter into another person's world without preconceived notions. Laying aside your views of yourself so as to enter into a transforming relationship will only occur when you feel secure enough within yourself. It is only then will you be able to maintain the person you have become. However, being empathetic is a complex and at times demanding way of living but it can also empower the person you are in a very subtle and gentle way.

Friendships that embrace empathy ensure that the people you engage with do not feel they are being judged. Further, the more your relationship with others is free of judgment and evaluation, the more it will permit the other person to realise and accept that they are really responsible for themselves.

To be able to establish these relationships of mutual trust, we need first of all to be true to ourselves. This requires us to accept ourselves as an imperfect human being who by no means functions at all times, in the way we would desire to function. The incredible paradox of this acceptance of self is that it is only when we truly accept the real 'me' that we will be capable of changing.

The depths of these relationships of honest engagement for many people can at times reach into the transcendental core of our very being. This can occur when our inner spirit reaches out to communicate with the inner spirit of another.

The core elements of these friendships depend on such strengths as 'empathy', which is the ability to understand the other person's condition and frame of reference. It is like walking in someone else's shoes. This requires checking out with the other person that you have correctly understood not only the spoken word, but also how they are truly feeling. This deep understanding is the most precious gift we can give to one another which is to be known as I know myself. Change can only take place if we believe we have been thoroughly understood and accepted for who we are.

The second important element of friendship is 'respect'. This requires responding to another in a way that conveys that you value the person for who they are, rather than what they may become. It requires the physical presence of closeness and the sense of joy that comes from a welcoming smile. We should never underestimate the power of a smile when greeting a friend. Valuing a person's personal space is also important while recognising at the same time physical closeness allows for confidential conversations. Leaning forward can also be understood as an act of intense listening. Listening is more than the passive activity of hearing because it may require action on your behalf.

In his book *Why don't people listen?* (p. 144), Hugh Mackay writes that if we really listen attentively then it is an, 'act of courage' because we run the risk of being influenced to change our minds on issues when we seriously entertain the ideas of another person. In his book On Becoming a Person, Carl Rogers wrote that, by seriously listening, you run the 'risk of being changed' yourself and this takes courage.

To be truly listened to is a precious gift especially from someone who is in effect saying, 'I am putting you first; I am going to entertain your ideas'. This is really listening.

Many year ago when I was being trained in the technique of Human Resource Development by using the Carkhuff and Berenson method, I discovered by accident the value of leaning forward while listening during a personal conversation, because leaning forward gave the person you are engaging with the feeling of really being listened to. These practice sessions were videotaped and when observing the tape later, people remarked on how attentive I was by leaning forward.

The reason this approach had become so natural to me was that I had a significant hearing loss and to hear what people were saying meant I needed to simply lean forward. The leaning forward communicated a sense of caring for the person, as well as positively regarding what the person were saying. It was my disability that had become a strength in the forming and maintaining of personal relationships.

The third significant element is recognising that most people are looking for practical ways of relating to their world and that they respond to people who have both feet on the ground. The most successful advice that a friend can give another is their experience in the practical activity of living, primarily because it makes sense with their own life experience.

The fourth issue is 'genuineness' which is of vital importance. Being genuine means you don't say things because you think it's the right thing to say but simply because you are actually living out in practice what you personally believe. The people who are your friends will respect and appreciate your honesty and in that way they will come to rely on the fact that what you say is who you really are. Being congruent is vitally important in establishing any long-term relationship.

The fifth major element is the importance of 'immediacy' in forming a positive relationship by being prepared to respond to the circumstances of the moment. By responding to the immediacy of the moment, you are recognising the importance of the reality of the current engagement and it confirms that you have been listening to and, more importantly, taking seriously the friendship.

The sixth important element in reinforcing a mutually open and honest friendship is not being afraid to confront the reality of what is happening. There is no value in denying that, at times, the possible consequences of an open relationship with someone who has become a friend. There are times when we just need to tell it as it is especially when one's words do not truly reflect our deepest feelings. It may take an invitation to examine closely our behaviour and, more importantly, a need for change if we desire an honest friendship to continue.

Being honest also requires us to affirm one another when we recognise the positive aspects of our relationship coming to the fore. I would argue that one of the greatest motivators in encouraging positive behaviour is for it to be recognised by someone you have a high regard for. So if you are grateful for the friendship, you need to let that person know.

The seventh crucial element of friendship is the recognition that we need at times to reveal our own experience in dealing with personal issues, which requires confronting the reality of our own feelings by laying them bare rather than by covering them up or denying their presence. This also may require explaining to your friend why these feelings affect you personally.

It is the quality and honesty of the friendship that encourages positive self-actualising growth to occur; further, in times of crisis, it is the quality of friendship that will protect you. It only takes one person to stand in solidarity with you at these times for healing to occur.

In times of great trauma when people are victimised because of race, gender, sexual orientation or religious belief, the power of friendship is so important. It is close personal friendships that confirm for us that we are responsible for each other and we can demonstrate this responsibility by standing with those who are being victimised.

There are many people who are suffering in our society today and we need to recognise that, through our friendships, we can provide the support that they require. It will take affirmative action on our part, whether it is a female friend suffering domestic violence, or an indigenous Australian being racially abused, or a homeless or refugee person seeking protection or shelter. It is the transforming power of friendship that will ensure that justice will prevail because of our support and advocacy.

During the time of the Nazi rule over Germany, the Lutheran pastor Martin Niemoeller was imprisoned in Dachau for seven years. During this time, while reflecting on the situation in Germany at this time, he wrote this following comment: 'When the Nazis came for the communists, I didn't speak up because I wasn't a communist. When they came for the Jews, I didn't speak up because I wasn't a Jew. Then they came for the trade unionists, but I didn't speak up because I wasn't a trade unionist. Then they came for the Catholics but I didn't speak up because I was a Protestant. Then they came for me and by that time there was no one to stand up for me.'

If we do not speak up about injustice as friends of those who are being abused then the oppressors will continue to create mayhem. In the words of Jewish writer, Professor and political activist Eli Wiesel: 'Always take sides. Neutrality helps the oppressor, never the victim. Silence encourages the tormentor never the tormented'.

The greatest test for any civilisation is how well it demonstrates its ability to include those who are different and to show compassion to those in need. The power of friendship is most influential in these circumstances, because it gives dignity through supportive advocacy to those who are suffering distress. The evidence clearly states that, 'A Just Society Depends on the Quality of Personal Relationships'.

In my teenage years, a friend was someone who shared similar interests and held similar values. It was someone you enjoyed spending time with to share life issues with each other. Today, many people no longer have friends they can hang out with, or who will visit them, even at times unannounced and when they appear they bring a deep sense of joy to your life. A friend was someone you could contact when you were feeling lonely because they would drop what they were doing to be with you.

These personal relationships depended on physical interaction, which is not possible through social media. As a teenager recently explained to me, 'The more I became involved in social media the more I craved personal interaction'. So the message clearly is: 'Make time to love people face-to-face not keyboard-to-keyboard'.

Chapter 3
The Way of the Historical Jesus

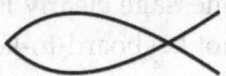

WHEN WE EXAMINE THE LIFE of Jesus of Nazareth, we discover that the ethical values he holds are expressed not only in his personal relationships, but also in his questioning of the authorities, be they political or religious. For those who are committed to a companionship with Jesus this is important to understand, because it means that we will at times need to challenge authorities, if their actions or policies disregard the importance of loving and compassionate relationships.

In a radio interview, Professor Lloyd Geering comes to a similar conclusion about the gospel writers' portrait of Jesus of Nazareth. He imagines that if Jesus had been listening to what they said about him he would not believe his ears. He most likely would have been appalled to hear that he considered himself as the only avenue to God, when we know how inclusive his attitude to life was. Jesus being 'the way, the truth and the life' or the 'light of the world' or the 'bread from heaven' or the 'Son of

God' was more a statement by the writer of John's Gospel than the actual words of Jesus. It is most likely that the interpretation of the so-called miracles would have been another source of irritation for Jesus, whether this was the miracle involving the control over nature or the feeding of the five thousand. The interpretation of the healing narratives and the formalising of the Jesus movement into a formal hierarchically structured church would not have met with Jesus' earnest endorsement.

It is most likely that there were times when people did not understand Jesus' humour, or his anger about injustice, or times when they misinterpreted his words and actions to justify their own behaviour.

We need to ask the question – who is the real Jesus?

If we accept that the personally transforming power of Jesus comes from his ability to form close interpersonal relationships then as followers of his way this is how we must respond to people we engage with.

The questions that arise for many followers of the Galilean sage are, 'Does Christian orthodoxy follow this path?' and 'Does the current policy, practice and beliefs of orthodoxy encourage interpersonal supportive and growth-promoting relationships?'

In an examination of the gospel narratives and the newly discovered sacred writings, we discover that Jesus has a belief in the inherent goodness of many of the people he encounters. However, what is it about Jesus that influences them? Is it only his words and his actions? The Jesus Seminar writers in analysing the 'voiceprint' of Jesus and placing these words and actions in their historical matrix give us a glimpse of this historical figure. I would add that people were attracted to Jesus as a result of this, but even more so people are attracted to Jesus because he made them feel worthwhile, included and valued. He conveyed a passion about life that was empowering. He was able to convey that he understood how people felt when they were devalued, or when they were excluded from their community, because of the laws associated with bodily functions that declared people unclean and unworthy to be embraced.

In John 13:34-35, we read the following – as translated by Professor Hal Taussig – 'I give you a new commandment – love one another, love one another as I have loved you. It is by this that everyone will recognise you as my followers – by loving one another'.

In Romans 12:9-11, the apostle Paul affirms the teaching of Jesus when he writes, 'Let your love be sincere. Hate the wrong, cling to the right. In the love of the community of the followers of Jesus, be affectionate to one another in showing respect, set an example of deference to one another'.

Did the words and actions of Jesus convey his emotions? When he wept at the death of his friend Lazarus who was the brother of Mary and Martha who were also friends of Jesus, and when he reached out to touch people who were unclean to welcome them with terms of endearment? Jesus made people aware of their worth by affirming that the spirit of sacred energy was within them and through recognising and drawing on this power they could accept themselves as people who are whole in the eyes of the God Spirit. Jesus offered a 'brokerless realm' in that people did not require a broker to communicate with God but were able to personally access this 'Sacred Spirit' because, as Jesus explained, it was within them.

Relationships that value us as worthwhile human beings can bring us to a sense of wholeness. Perhaps the question we need to ask is not, 'What did we understand about the experience of an embracing relationship?' but 'How did this relationship make us feel?' By changing our image of ourselves, we can embrace life with a passion and see real value in those we meet.

I hope that theological students ask themselves the question, 'How do I feel about this? What effect does this have on me emotionally?' I don't want to hear so much what they think the parable means, but more importantly how it makes them feel. I would want to ask: are you angry, sad, excited about what can be done to make this a better world? Theological students need to experience the emotions expressed by the disciples on the road to Emmaus when they proclaimed, 'Were not our hearts burning within us while he was talking to us on the road...' (Luke 24:32) Or, like John Wesley, is their heart strangely warmed when spending time listening to Jesus? Relationships are about emotions and feelings that commit us to action. It is not so much a debate about what Barth, or Tillich, would say, but what was it that moved them to commit their lives to modelling their behaviour on this man Jesus.

Faith is about the important things of life that 'move' us, such as love, friendships, justice and, most of all, passion and compassion. This is what makes us who we are. These are the things that Jesus the 'wisdom sage' conveys. What is it that compels you to risk your life? Is it science, mathematics, engineering or is it a passion for living in a better world?

The historical Jesus message is not about satisfying one's ego, it is about unconditional love instead of revenge. Jesus' life is about living life abundantly, it was a life grounded in a commitment to freeing people to love wastefully and to travel beyond their boundaries and their fears, regardless of their race, social status, ethnicity or gender.

Or as Henri Nouwen has stated, 'For Jesus, there are no countries to be conquered, no ideologies to be imposed, no people to be dominated. There are only children, women and men to be loved'. For those who understand this message it will transform their lives, because it takes 'humanity' to a totally new dimension. It transforms the purpose of life from a preoccupation with self-preservation to one of universal interconnectedness, which embraces an awareness of the sacred connectedness of all things.

Jesus would have been shocked and dismayed to hear that people considered him to be the 'Messiah'. He would have seen this as an anathema. His principal message is that the sacred power we call GOD resides within each of us providing us with the energy and wisdom to take responsibility for our own wholeness.

Jesus embodied a way of life that accepted the realities of existence and pointed to another way, a fuller way – an abundant way of responding to the reality we experience. To be humane requires that together we strive to alleviate human suffering. To be humane is to live the abundant life that Jesus envisioned and this requires us to live by the values Jesus espoused. Are our personal values challenged when we compare them with the values Jesus holds?

We need to stop looking for the intervention of a Messianic figure and realise that the power to change the world lies within us. When Jesus affirms people by telling them that their faith has made them whole, he is confirming his message of the God Spirit within us.

Jesus has a belief in the inherent goodness of people. Jesus' life is about living abundantly, it was a life grounded in a commitment to freeing people to love wastefully beyond their boundaries and their fears regardless of their race, ethnicity or gender.

Each Sunday morning when I attend church, I hear the words of the hymns, or listen to the prayers and the sermon, but I do not have the urgent impulse to go outside and shout aloud to the community that I am alive because of a sacred spirit within me. At the end of the church service, my pulse is not racing and I certainly do not feel that I am walking on a cloud.

And why is this so? I firmly believe it is because what I have been listening to and singing is a message 'about' Jesus, and not the Message 'of' Jesus. This dilemma is further compounded because, in most cases the message I hear about Jesus does not depict the Historical Jesus of Nazareth I have come to know through my reading of the gospels.

What then do I mean by the term 'the message of Jesus'? The paramount message of the human Jesus is that the kingdom of God is 'immanent' and is, as he claims in Luke 17:21 'among you'. The term kingdom of God or kingdom of heaven are mentioned one hundred and eight times in the canonical gospels alone. The Greek term 'Basileia' has been translated as kingdom of God or kingdom of heaven in the *New Revised Standard Version* of the Bible. However, recent New Testament scholarship explains that a more appropriate translation would be 'imperial rule', because it is about what kings and tyrants do and hence it is a verb and not a noun. It is about 'power' and 'rule', which infers a process rather than a place – a way of life more than a location.

Why do I declare this message to be a radical one? Simply because this message challenges the traditional image of God held by the Jews in the time of Jesus. The image of God, which was influenced by the sacred writings of the Old Testament such as Daniel (7:22-27), had three essential elements that were proclaimed by John the Baptist in Matthew's Gospel (3:7-10). These three essential elements are first, that God will visit earth very soon, and it is imminent. Secondly, the timing of this visit relies entirely on when God chooses to intervene, so the God of the Jews is an interventionist God. Thirdly, this intervention will be accompanied with divine violence. God of Judaism is a powerful, violent, interventionist deity, and this intervention is imminent. God will not only judge the kingdoms of the world because they have failed to heed the warnings of the chosen people, God will also judge the Jews for failing to heed the call to repentance.

The 'radical' nature of the Jesus message is more easily understood in Jesus' teaching parables where he likens the kingdom of God to a 'mustard seed' is a parable we find in Luke 13:18-19. Here, Jesus confronts his audience with a provocative image suggesting that God's domain is like an uncontrollable garden weed. A weed that has the ability to take over the whole garden and it is this dangerous 'take control' quality that ensures its survival, even in the harshest environments. Jesus is saying that once you let God into your life, it is quite possible that God will take over and you will no longer be in control.

However, it is the parable of the yeast that appeals most to me because it depicts that the spiritual energy source we call God is in all things, hidden yet apparent, not ostentatious, but quietly working in all types of situations. Unlike Jewish tradition, Jesus is declaring that God is everywhere present with us now. It is interesting to note that Jesus tells his audience that a woman actually hides, or, more correctly, 'conceals' the leaven in the bread. This is a provocative statement from Jesus because the Jews, through their celebration of the Passover, eat only unleavened bread, and regard leaven as symbol of 'corruption'. This raises the question: is the message of God proclaimed by Jesus one aimed at corrupting society, and if so what is our role as followers?

The new paradigm proposed by Jesus regarding the kingdom of God is a clear indication that he believed God was present in human life and was as close as one's heart beat. As he says in Luke's Gospel 'it is amongst you, but people do not see it'. As followers of Jesus, our task is to recognise the signs of the 'kingdom' and to reveal and affirm them. They may be in the random acts of kindness or a generosity of spirit that we witness in the lives of those whom we make contact with everyday, where each reveals the sacred activity we call God. If the kingdom of

God is within you, then God comes to visibility in your relationships with others.

The second vital point of this message regarding God's presence is that it is not an interventionist one from a powerful deity, but a collaborative one. We can perceive in the life of Jesus a source of spiritual energy that he is not forced into relying on, but actively chooses to do so, because it gives him a sense of wholeness. We too can empower each other through inclusion, unconditional acceptance and positive regard, which are the fruits that give visibility to the presence of God. It is possible to experience a spiritual presence within us by working together collaboratively.

The third significant feature of the Jesus message is that the God of Jesus is 'non-violent'. Jesus presents us with a sacred energy source that can transform the world, not through violent intervention, but through love. Jesus had the skill to effect quite radical change through the use of parody, non-compliance, humour and exaggeration. He did not practise 'passive resistance' but 'active non-violent resistance'.

The message that I want to hear from the church is the message that Jesus proclaimed himself, which affirms that a non-interventionist, non-violent and collaborative God abides within and between us, and when we discern it in the lives of people around us, we must proclaim it for what it is and affirm it. The kingdom of God comes (as the Our Father prayer affirms) when we empower each other to live fully, love wastefully, and be all that we are capable of being. We have been given the God-given power to be a spiritually defiant, beloved community, of resistance to the evils of this world. If we achieve this, it will quicken the pulse.

For those who understand this message, it transforms their life, because it takes 'humanity' to a totally new dimension. It transforms the purpose of life from 'self-preservation' to a 'universal interconnectedness' with an awareness of the sacred 'Spirit' that connects all things. Jesus does have a vision of what the world should accept as vital, if people are to live positive and fulfilled lives. Jesus refers to this vision as God's domain or realm, which he affirms is present within and between the lives of his disciples and all people.

This is a realm that Jesus did not create or control, it was present before he was born. We find that in the 'healing narratives' where Jesus states six times that a person's healing comes from the sacred energy that resides within and is not because of his person or influence. Nor does healing have to wait until Jesus is crucified.

This is the vision that Jesus is asking his disciples to affirm and it also includes all who value their friendship with Jesus today. His original disciples, like us today, unfortunately continued to stare at his finger and not at where that finger was pointing. Jesus' vision was of a world where peace, justice and compassion is expressed in our relationships with others and it is this that would bring about 'God's Realm' as defined by the gospel writers.

Perhaps the translation of the Greek *basileia tou Theou* does not truly reflect what Jesus means by the 'kingdom of God'. Most scholars agree that Jesus' native tongue was Aramaic not Greek and according to O'Murchu 2017, the most likely word used by Jesus would have been the Aramaic *Malkuta*. This is important because unlike the Greek and English notion of kingdom with all its imperial connotation of top down authority and obedience, the word 'Malkuta' denotes a concept of mutual empowerment, where power is equally shared and dispensed for the benefit of the receiver rather than the giver. Hence, the 'kingdom of God' as defined by Jesus is a realm of radical inclusion and a community of radical equality where each has the power to engage with the sacred Spiritual energy we call God.

This definition of the 'kingdom' fits well with Dominic Crossan's concept that the 'kingdom' is in reality a 'companionship of empowerment'. So the call to 'seek first the kingdom of God' is Jesus calling us to share in the 'companionship of empowerment' because in this companionship we will find that it is the 'relational' activities that truly liberates, nurtures and leads us to a life of wholeness. It is not only in the words of Jesus; it is also in his actions that we understand the importance of a personal response to others.

For example, Jesus practises 'Open Commensality' or more simply open table, which is translated from the Latin *mensa* meaning table; here, everyone is invited to share the meal with equal status. The concept of open commensality honours people for who they are as relational human beings and in this sense it is radically egalitarian. According to Dominic Crossan in his book *Jesus a Revolutionary Biography* (p. 71), 'Open Commensality is the symbol and embodiment of radical egalitarianism, of an absolute equality of people that denies the validity of any discrimination between them and negates the necessity of any hierarchy among them'.

The stranger is not simply tolerated, but respected and is welcomed at the table. So perhaps it is time for us all to reclaim the message of Jesus as opposed to the message of churchianity. This can be achieved, by removing the hierarchical images of God and Jesus and replacing them with our human ability to show compassion to all and by so doing we will reveal the spirit of God within all people as Jesus did with his friends. Then the spirit of the sacred energy we call God will be revealed in the way we care for each other.

If we follow the lead offered by Jesus, then we become in Crossan's terms, 'companions in empowerment' because, as the story in the Old Testament of Ruth illustrates, it is through her steadfast loyalty that the offer of love and acceptance from Naomi is returned in even greater measure, when Ruth proclaims:

> Where you go, I will go;
> where you lodge, I will lodge;
> your people shall be my people,
> and your God my God' (Ruth 1:16).

Ruth was an outsider – she was a Moabite, or, in today's terms, she was one of 'them', but Naomi needed her for the completeness of her character as much as Ruth needed Naomi for the fulfilment of hers.

This is also the Jesus vision. For Jesus, it is not just a matter of healing but of 'liberation', and this is achieved through relationships of embrace. Would you be a friend and most of all a companion of Jesus? A number of Progressives no longer call themselves Christians, primarily because of the bad press this term has received by the people who lay claim to this title. Some people will refer to themselves as 'friends of Jesus' making the distinction between the way of Jesus and the behaviour of those who are members of Christian orthodoxy.

The life of Jesus was not about religion but, about embracing life with gratitude and a passion. He called on those around him to seize the opportunities that life presented as stated in John 10:10 'I have come that you might have life and have more abundantly'. Jesus embraced life with a passion and lived accordingly – he was willing to seize the day – *'carpe diem'*.

In an examination of the gospel narratives and the newly discovered sacred writings found at Nag Hammadi, we discover that Jesus has a belief in the inherent goodness of people. The message of Jesus and his belief in the inherent goodness of people is based on the personal values he holds, and we witness these values when we analyse his words and actions.

First, let us examine the value of 'compassion'. In chapter 4, I defined compassion as 'A feeling of distress and pity for the suffering and misfortune of another, often including the desire to alleviate it'.

How then did Jesus display the value of compassion? We need first to recognise that compassionate love is counter-culture, because it creates upheavals in the way we understand ourselves, as well as others and even the world around us. Also compassion does not alleviate suffering, but it does transform it because it helps us experience what injustice feels like.

Compassion signifies standing in solidarity with another's suffering, feeling within ourselves something of the other's pain and trauma. The English definition of compassion as a noun means to suffer together with. In the words of Karen Armstrong (2011) 'Despite various nuances of the word, compassion it is the most outstanding unifying force among the world's religions. It is the active living out of the universal desire to love unconditionally'.

In Armstrong's *Charter of Compassion*, she concludes, that compassion is essential to human relationships and it fulfils humanity. For Armstrong compassion is the path to enlightenment, and indispensable in the creation of a just economy and a peaceful global community. This definition of compassion denotes a social power that underpins harmony, solidarity, and a non-violent power for healing and peace. This force is also a political value that can foster economic and structural justice. However, most importantly this definition of compassion as a verb reinforces 'inclusiveness'.

If this form of compassion were released freely into our world, then it would most likely remove or at least alleviate the majority of the social evils that will be outlined in chapter 6. The reason this has not occurred is because so often the feelings of compassion do not translate into practical action as they do in the life, words and actions of Jesus the Galilean sage. In the gospels, the word compassion denotes a great deal more than purely feelings or emotion. Compassion in the New Testament is, in reality, a bold subversive claim for justice, liberation and empowerment.

In gospel terms, compassion is not simply a feeling of mercy or pity because these terms can evoke a patronising concern rather than the commitment to positive action. The word compassion used in the gospels comes from the Greek word *splangnezomai* which literally means 'being moved from the depths of one's bowels' (O'Murchu, 2015). This term then is about the quality of an active response to rectify the wrong being felt or perceived, and this comes as a result of an inner enlightenment that seeks empowerment as a resolution to human suffering. In reality, it is a pursuit of justice.

In the New Testament, the word for compassion occurs seventeen times and is applied to Jesus on eight occasions. When the term is applied to Jesus, it is the form of a verb and not a noun. In other words, for Jesus, compassion is not simply a feeling of pity, it is a quality that requires action to right a wrong. Compassion then is about what a person feels compelled to do, and not only the concern they feel for the suffering of another.

This understanding of compassion by Jesus is summarised in his quote in Luke's Gospel 6:36. 'Be compassionate as your Father God is compassionate'. This call from Jesus flies in the face of the Judaic call in Leviticus 19:2 'You shall be holy for I the Lord your God am holy', which claims that purity is more important than compassion. Jesus' emphasis on compassion rather than on purity is a radical change from Orthodox Judaism.

In his book *Meeting Jesus Again for the First Time*, Marcus Borg confirms that for Jesus the key component that fashioned his life was active compassion. It is more than a quality of God – it is the base value for life lived in community. Jesus is committed to living inclusively rather than adhering to some formal religion.

How did Jesus see himself was it as a 'suffering servant' or did he see himself as a 'liberator'? I could find no evidence to suggest that Jesus saw himself as a substitutionary sacrifice; in fact, there is evidence to the contrary when we read Luke 4:18-19. Here Jesus reads from Isaiah 61:1-2 which states:

> The Spirit of the Lord is upon me, because he has anointed me to bring good news to the poor. He has sent me to proclaim release to the captives and recovery of sight to the blind, to let the oppressed go free, to proclaim the year of the Lord's favour.

If Jesus understood his role to be one of sacrifice, we would assume he would have read from the beginning of Isaiah 53 which speaks of being 'wounded for our transgressions'.

Jesus does not portray God as a punishing vindictive deity, but as a loving parent. Jesus does not see God as a blood-lusting deity who demands a ransom to sooth a wounded pride, and Jesus did not speak of his life as being a sacrifice.

When we examine this event in the Nazareth Synagogue, it reveals that Luke has combined traditions from a variety of sources to compose a scenario for Jesus to visit his hometown. The composition seems to lack clarity and does not flow; however, it does illustrate well, both the positive and negative aspects of his homecoming. There is nothing unusual in what Jesus does; he is gathering together with his fellow Jews on the Sabbath in the synagogue. And as was the custom in the first century as a visiting Rabbi, he was invited to read from the traditional texts and to speak.

The immediate reaction to Jesus' reading from Isaiah is one of praise, 'All spoke well of him and were amazed at the gracious words that came from his mouth'. (Luke 4:22). Then a doubt begins to arise among them: 'Is this not Joseph's son?' Is this not Jesus the carpenter's son?

In the Mediterranean world 2000 years ago, a son takes up the profession of his father and receives the name of his grandfather. If Jesus' father is an artisan then, why is he preaching and teaching, rather than working with his hands, as he should. The reaction of the people in the Synagogue is a natural human response, not justified maybe, but natural. In our own experience in the Australian Christian Church, we look more often for scholarship first from the USA, or the UK, before recognising our local talent.

It seems that Jesus has anticipated their rejection and he delivers an insulting put down to their yet unvoiced objection. 'Truly I tell you no prophet is accepted in the prophets' own home town.' The insult is sharpened further when Jesus claims that Gentile strangers are better able to judge the honour of a prophet than those who know him on a daily basis (vv. 25-27). Their anger turns to rage and they chase him with the intent of throwing him over a cliff if they catch him, but he manages to slip away from them.

What is really wonderful about this text is that for Jesus belief and action are not separate. For Jesus to believe that he had been anointed to bring good news to the poor, release to the captives, sight to the blind and freedom to the oppressed, then, he could do no other than express this regardless of the consequences. Further, that Jesus sees these as matters for the whole community and not just the church. Perhaps, this is a lesson we still need to learn today?

Perhaps, one of the greatest difficulties for Christians is our reluctance to take the message of the gospels seriously and apply that message to our daily lives. We have a wonderful ability to block out those portions of scripture that challenge our prejudices and would prompt us to action outside our comfort zone.

For example, a question much ignored these days is whether our faith has anything to do with justice, consumerism, poverty and other socio-political issues. The Uniting Church in Australia, through the Synod Commissions and to a lesser extent the Presbytery committees, raises social justice issues but the dilemma has always been how we can get this message across to congregations. There is a yawning gap between the world of our faith and the world of action that involves the real issues at the local level. As Christians, will we ever question the need to change our behaviour or to confront our culture?

Groups often linked to evangelical values provide confirmation of this ability to block out the social justice aspects of the gospel. What are the issues that are associated with the powerful Christian coalitions of the USA? Forgiveness? Responding to those who live in poverty? Liberty for the captives? Setting the oppressed free? Caring for the wounded? Are the high profile members of the Church concerned also about the effects of consumerism?

We hear them make pronouncements about moral decay of our society; we hear them trumpet their own particular enlightenment as the only way to God. We hear them condemn people with AIDS as those who are incurring the wrath of God. We hear them make pronouncements about the morality of homosexuals by reference to some obscure text whilst ignoring the message of inclusivity shown by Jesus of Nazareth.

To understand the values that Jesus embraces we need first of all to examine the words and actions attributed to him from the sacred writings and to closely analyse what these stories tell us about Jesus' values. The gospels tell us that Jesus analysed and reviewed his values through the process of the spiritual activity of contemplation.

The term 'room' – as it is used in the gospels – when viewed as a metaphor, means 'time out' for reflection, contemplation and meditation. It is not what we read or hear but what these messages make us feel compelled to do. Passion changes the world because it has the power to change us. I believe the term 'go into your room' is being used by Jesus 'metaphorically'. Of this I believe we can be virtually certain. Jesus was a mystic, a contemplative, and this is the approach to spirituality that he taught. My colleague and friend Lorraine Parkinson confirmed this when she explained that Jesus would have been familiar with the accounts of Moses at the burning bush, Elijah hearing the 'still small voice', Samuel claiming to hear One 'calling' to him in the middle of the night; many of the psalms are deeply 'contemplative' also.

The clue to Jesus' own spirituality lies in his saying, 'When you pray, go into your room, shut the door and pray to your father who is in secret'. For Jesus, 'real' prayer was an intensely private matter. I think the clue is in that word translated 'room'. In our Greek version, it means an inner storage chamber or even a secret room. Working backwards to the Aramaic, which was probably used by Jesus, this would likely have been 'tumaya' – a secret place where valuables were kept. It could be used metaphorically for your innermost being or in other words it could be translated as, contemplation, introspection, requiring going inwards.

The Jewish method of inwardly contemplating known as 'Teshuva' as referred to earlier is quite possibly the method of contemplation that Jesus used, which is a very personal, deep and meaningful process, which requires considerable contemplation and reflection and a preparedness to make changes to the way one relates to others.

An important value of Jesus is his commitment to personal justice. This is demonstrated in his commitment to the sharing of meals with others in what has been described as 'Open Commensality' which is translated from the Latin *mensa* meaning table.

This value is demonstrated in his parable of the 'feeding of the five thousand' as described in John, chapter 6. 'Then Jesus took the loaves, and when he had given thanks, he distributed them to those who were seated; so also the fish, as much as they wanted.' In John 6:11, it is interesting to recognise that only one miracle makes it into all four gospels and it is the feeding of the five thousand. It occurs on a grassy hill on the shores of the Sea of Galilee at a time when Jesus popularity was cresting. Wherever he went, people were demanding his attention, for wisdom and for healing.

Whilst reflecting on this gospel message, I was struck by the parallel between Jesus' act of distribution of the fish and loaves and his actions at the last supper where he refers to himself as bread and wine, body and blood. The last supper is conducted with just the disciples but this ceremony is conducted with the general community. Is it possible that the loaves and fish symbolise the elements of Jesus' acceptance and embrace of people even more than the elements of bread and wine. Look at the similarities: Jesus takes bread, blesses it or give thanks and then breaks it and distributes it to the people.

A brief investigation reveals that there are paintings on the walls of the earliest Christian catacombs, dating from slightly before 200 AD, that characteristically depict seven or eleven male figures, presumably apostles, seated at a table, about to partake of two fish and five loaves. We know also how important the sign of the fish was to the early Christians, particularly those who were under persecution. It was a sign of belonging. In early Christian funerary carvings and inscriptions, we find the two fish and five loaves depicted there also.

It appears, therefore, that two different traditions developed, one of bread and fish, another of bread and wine, symbolically ritualised after Jesus' death to recognise the openness of his embrace for all people. There have been many attempts to explain the parable of the feeding of the five thousand such as the boy's act of giving all that he has shames the others into revealing the food they had kept hidden under their garments. OR that Jesus gave each a crumb similar to our Eucharist feast and they were filled, because of the act of sharing. Some say that Jesus had the power to multiply the food as he distributed it; but I am not sure that these reasons for explaining the event are important. What is important is the meaning of the story for the Christian community. I believe this story to be a 'metaphor' that conveys an important egalitarian message and it is this: 'if we are willing to share what we have, there will not only be enough to go round to all present, there will also be some left over which we can share with those in need'.

Like many people, some of the greatest experiences in my life have been enjoying conversations around a good meal and a bottle of wine. I can close my eyes and recall places and people who have lifted my spirits or challenged me to be more honest with myself or more coherent with my thoughts and actions. These times I will always treasure, be it eating abalone and black bean sauce in Kota Kinabalu, or a Greek salad in Santorini.

How many times does Jesus use the meal to engage people? How often does Jesus dismiss the rules of society to make people feel welcome? How often does he challenge people to participate in community through a common meal? These activities are used to encourage people to understand that they belong together and that they are considered worthy through the sharing of some very personal experiences; we are able to experience the fullness of the Spirit that binds us together as we embrace each other.

What can happen when we commit ourselves to the possibility of relationships is we risk not only revealing ourselves but we also risk entering into a relationship of care. By Jesus' actions, he is telling us we belong to each other and we are responsible for each other; he reveals this by the way he shares his time in the ordinary things of life, such as meal times. The Eucharist tells us that we are one with Jesus and we are one with each other and this is the message of the gospel – 'we belong together, to share with each other; yes even to feel each other's pain'. Jesus is clear about the priorities of life.

It is also a message about the priorities of sharing equally with one another because it is more important than seeking our own personal glory. However, we seem to be more concerned about the *Goods and Services Tax*, or the *Mandatory Sentencing Laws*, or our refusal to say sorry to our indigenous sisters and brothers; than we are about their well-being, their health, housing, welfare and education.

The example of the life of Jesus is confronting us with need to get our priorities right. The values of Jesus encourage us to accept and embrace each other and to share in open commensality not only our food, but also our very selves. This is the meaning of discipleship, to allow the spirit that moves Jesus to work within us for he 'has the power to accomplish abundantly far more than we can imagine'.

Jesus' personal values are demonstrated in the gospels; first, let us examine Jesus and his response to the equality of women. The human activities of Jesus such as in his response to the rights of women is revealed in a number of gospel stories. Women were an integral component of Jesus entourage as we read in Luke 8:1-3 'The twelve were with him, as well as some women who had been cured of evil spirits and infirmities'.

One of stories about Jesus' response to people seeking healing is of the woman who has been haemorrhaging for twelve years. I will also include briefly the story of Jairus' daughter because both these stories are interwoven in more ways than one. This story can be found, with variations, in three gospels Matthew 9:18–26, Mark 5:21–43, and Luke 8:40–56. I will attempt to interpret this story from the perspective of a Jesus seminar scholar and further consider the implications of this interpretation from a 'practice' perspective. First, let us quickly re-cap this story.

We begin with Jesus walking with one of the elders of the synagogue a man named Jairus, a leader in the community. They are heading to his house because his daughter is sick and Jesus has been asked to heal her. On their journey, they are surrounded by a large crowd and as these people begin to press in, Jesus experiences a special contact with a woman who has been haemorrhaging for twelve years. The number twelve is significant in that Jairus daughter is said to be twelve years of age.

As a result of the woman's touch, Jesus stops what he is doing to respond to the woman's need, and whilst he is speaking to her he hears of the child's death. Undeterred, he continues to the house of Jairus and announces that the girl is not 'dead' but sleeping and he recommends she be given food.

Let us now examine more closely the situation concerning this woman who has been haemorrhaging for twelve years. Keeping in mind that Jesus has a reputation for sharing meals and time with all new comers including unattached women; so his direct response to a woman would not be considered out of character. However, it would have caused consternation for those around him, especially his disciples. In reality, Jesus condemns the world of exclusion, because he does not condemn the woman for her actions. His acceptance of her is demonstrated by his use of the term 'daughter'. His words affirm that her blood flow doesn't make her unclean. The 'purity laws' are themselves false boundaries that marginalise her and stand in the way for her healing to occur. If healing is to be successful, she will require the support of friends and family and she will need to be included in her community.

It is important for people who are seeking healing to feel that they are in what Dietrich Bonhoeffer in his 1937 book *The Cost of Discipleship* refers to as a 'State of Grace'; that they belong, and they are people of worth and as a result they are valued. The woman in this story is being denied a 'state of grace' as well as being excluded from the nurturing, personal and social activities that come from intimate contact. For twelve years, she had been haemorrhaging. For twelve years she had been considered unclean by her faith community; not only is she unclean, everything she touches she makes unclean including the clothes that Jesus is wearing. Her touch makes Jesus unclean. Her partner, her children, the bed she slept on, her clothes, her cooking utensils are all contaminated by her declared state of being 'unclean'. As sexual relationships are forbidden during this time it is quite conceivable that her partner has left her and that her family and friends have abandoned her.

To understand this situation, we may find it valuable to imagine what it would be like to be this person, what would this condition mean to you as a human being? Just for a minute, imagine what it would be like to spend a whole day without being touched, without being held gently and lovingly, without being caressed. Now try to imagine how you would feel if you went a week or a month without being touched. Now imagine what it would be like to go through twelve long years of isolation; living without embrace. Forget for a moment the isolating effect of the 'purity laws'; consider for a moment how this woman would be feeling physically as well as psychologically. In all likelihood, her iron count would be quite low, bringing with it a loss of energy and a debilitating tiredness, which only compounds her feelings of isolation. She must have felt exhausted and incredibly alone and quite possibly depressed.

To make matters worse, in Mark's account we read that she has spent money on physicians but to no avail. Under the temple cult, she would have been urged to purify herself by bathing in the pools just outside the temple and for this she would have to pay the priestly authorities. However, her search for a cure had only left her in a state of poverty (common today among people with chronic illness or disability), additional to her state of distress through the marginalisation and shame.

In the depth of despair, her search for healing becomes so desperate that she embarks on this risky venture. She has obviously heard of the healing power of this man, Jesus of

Nazareth, and so with the protection of the crowd she comes up to him from behind and touches his clothes. It is possible that she believed this act in itself would be sufficient and then she could melt back into the crowd and return home. It does appear that she believed by this very act – that of touching his clothes – she would receive healing. But what an incredible risk this woman takes just by being in a crowd in her state of ritual impurity. She takes an even greater risk by reaching out to touch Jesus. Regardless of her condition just being a woman in the society of this day she would be shamed, simply by touching a male stranger without his consent, and without being introduced to him by a male friend or member of her family.

Touching Jesus' clothes is the same as touching his person; both his clothes and his person are now impure. Jesus being a Jew would have been aware of this fact.

This is a desperate act but if she doesn't have a male friend to intercede for her, is there an option? If she were to shout 'unclean', 'unclean', the crowd would have prevented her from getting close. She has nothing to lose by taking this form of action. She is already treated as if she were non-existent; in fact her church and her society have made her 'dead'. It is interesting to note that young menstruating women were also considered 'dead' by their family and society. In his book *Christianity's Dangerous Memory*, Diarmuid O'Murchu suggests that Jairus' daughter may have been experiencing her first menstruation and when Jesus requests that she be given something to eat, it is possible that he is instructing the family that she eat with them at their table. In so doing, they are including her back into the embrace of the family.

What is Jesus' reaction to the desperate action of this bold and assertive woman? He stops what he is doing and responds to the woman's dilemma. He responds to her by calling her 'daughter' a term of endearment and by so doing recognises her as a person of worth. Jesus offers her something that she has craved for twelve years –a relationship with another human being. Jesus then says, 'Daughter, your faith has made you well: go in peace and be healed of your disease' (Mark 5:34). In making the statement, 'Your faith has made you well', Jesus is giving the woman credit for the healing, rather than claiming credit for himself. In his book *Problems With the Atonement*, Stephen Finlan emphasises the theological point that healing is not dependent on the death of Jesus.

If Jesus claims, 'Your faith has made you whole', which he does six times in the healing narratives, then at that point you are whole. The healing experience is already available. Jesus doesn't say, 'after my soon to occur death you will be healed and only after I am dead will you be made whole'. Thus, Jesus doesn't see salvation or healing as being dependent on his sacrificial death, Jesus at no time requests the woman to believe in him as 'Saviour' before announcing she has been made whole; nor does he make this request in other healing narratives.

Remember the story of a woman who comes uninvited to the house of Simon the Pharisees bringing with her an expensive jar of perfumed ointment. Jesus, in the custom of the day, is reclining on the cushions at the banquet. Hence, she approaches him from behind and begins to anoint his feet with the ointment and her tears and not only does she dry his feet with her hair, she also kisses his feet.

This story in one form or another is recorded in the four canonical gospels. Each story has its own particular emphasis regarding the place, the people present, and the particular moment in Jesus' ministry. It doesn't matter if this woman is a local prostitute, or if she is Mary sister of Lazarus, the act of kindness is the same and the response from Jesus is the same. To some extent so is the reaction of the observers, as they attempt to place negative connotations on interpreting why this act of love is being carried out.

Jesus understands the woman's need for acceptance; she is seeking recognition from a person she respects and in return she is welcomed with dignity as well as respect. Note Jesus' words, 'She has shown great love' or 'She has done something beautiful'.

Jesus is able to accept what this woman offers as a way of seeking connection without condemning her past behaviour. He does not say, 'Depart from me, you wicked temptress, because you are a wicked and evil person and your soul shall rot in hell for the sins you have committed'.

When Jesus uses the phrase, 'Your faith has saved you', as referred to earlier, it is not just a one off comment. When we examine these words more closely, we first note that they are in past tense, indicating that the action of being saved has already happened and that its' results continue into the present. Hence when Jesus says to this woman 'Your faith has saved you', he is saying, 'by your contrition and humble act of loving kindness, you have revealed that the spirit of God is with you'. She is already in a relationship with God and her compassionate actions display the fruits of this relationship. It is the Spirit of God that has already reached into her life and it is because of this she has the potential to be made whole.

Jesus believes wholeness is freely available without any mediating transaction, and faith means trusting in God's straightforward generosity, and forgiveness is conditioned only by one's willingness to forgive others.

If my interpretation of this text is correct, then it changes significantly how we have understood the relationship between the person seeking wholeness and God. Further, it places in question the role of Jesus' death as the only avenue for people seeking a relationship with God. When Jesus proclaims, 'Your faith has saved you', he changes the relationship with the sacred from one of master/servant to one of a 'companionship of empowerment'.

This story is a beautiful metaphor about liberation and wholeness but, more importantly, it is about the power of the sacred Spirit to enter into people's lives and to offer them wholeness without any demand for a sacrificial offering.

We have another story in John 8:3–4 where Jesus is called on not only to judge a woman but to give approval for her stoning to death. The authorities are trying to trap Jesus about how he would respond to some poor woman who was caught in the act of adultery. The authorities saw it as their chance to stone a woman to death for adultery, and also to be able to charge Jesus with religious disloyalty.

Jesus' response is compassionate because he bends forward and begins to trace something on the ground for the woman's eyes only, and then he challenges those who have gathered around about who has the moral right to cast the first stone. It is possible that if most of those gathered are men, then maybe they were confronted by Jesus' challenge in such a way that it made them realise that it is often men who are largely responsible for sexual crimes. Slowly, they all move away leaving Jesus alone with the woman.

Jesus is offering a new understanding of God as one who is not judgmental but one who is compassionate. This is a very radical message. Jesus addresses this woman tenderly and respectfully by calling her 'woman'. Then he asked if there was anyone left to condemn her and she replies, 'No one'. Jesus realises that this woman needs reassurance and not condemnation so he also replies, 'Neither do I condemn you'. In today's world in which women are treated so violently, this really is a radical message.

The human activities of Jesus such as in his response to the rights of women is revealed in a number of gospel stories. It needs to also be realised that women were an integral component of Jesus entourage as we read in Luke 8:1–3 'The twelve were with him, as well as some women who had been cured of evil spirits and infirmities'.

Jesus also calls us to love our neighbours as ourselves. In Luke, chapter 10, we have the story of the 'Good Samaritan', which is at the heart of the gospel message, because it encourages us to understand in practical terms the meaning of this message of Jesus. The distinctive nature of the Jesus Movement is to pronounce the presence of the kingdom. God's kingdom in this parable is defined by radical egalitarianism, which is demonstrated by Jesus and his disciples through 'open commensality' and 'healing'. We need to explore the God Jesus knew before Christianity clothed him in religious language.

If we believe that Jesus of Nazareth presents a positive, inclusive, loving God, then how should we respond, and how should we act when confronted with a needy situation? The story of the Good Samaritan gives us an example of what the inclusion of all people in the healing process means. Jesus as a response to the question 'who is my neighbour?' told this story. It is often called the story of the 'Good Samaritan' but for many Jews the term 'Good Samaritan' is an oxymoron.

Let us now recap this story. It is important to note the long description that is given to the actions of the Samaritan which is greater than any other elements of the story – 66 words more, but why? Great care has been taken to describe the goodness of the Samaritan to the hearers because they would be sceptical. The greatest emphasis is on the doer not what is done simply because it would not be expected that a Samaritan businessman would respond with such compassion toward a Jew.

The first thing we are confronted with in this story is that the love of God does not simply merge with the love of our neighbour; Jesus does not simply make it a means or passage to the love of God. We have to love the other person for their own sake, not because it is a condition of a loving God.

In this story, the Samaritan responds to the person who has been beaten and robbed, simply because this person is in need. This story is told with the greatest care because, as we are told, the Samaritan binds up his wounds, he alleviates his pain, and he sets the sick man on his beast and brings him to an inn and puts him in the care of the innkeeper. He pays for the initial expenses and promises to make good any further expense, when he comes back this way.

Note how simply and without sentimentality the Samaritan is described: the shrewd merchant, practical and careful with his means and money, someone who would do nothing that is not necessary at the time. Jesus tells this story with no parade of 'religion'. It is clear that the Samaritan is not a religious man. What he does is aimed at the sufferer with no side-glances at God; he is not looking over his shoulder to see if God is watching. The Samaritan does not ask 'Are you watching, God? Will you mark this in your great book. On the day of judgment, will you mark this act as a plus?'

Jesus is asking us to respond primarily because we are moved with compassion, not because we want to be noticed by God. In Matthew 25:31ff, Jesus tells of the final judgment which explains that we will all be judged for how we have responded with love to one another because, in so doing we have responded to Jesus himself. This message clearly tells us we must be prepared for God's call, which will come to us in the person of our neighbour. As Mother Teresa claims, 'Each of them (the poor in the street, the 'unclean') is really Jesus in disguise'.

Who then is our neighbour? The story of the 'Good Samaritan' is Jesus' response to this question. To answer this question, we must put ourselves in the position of the person who has been beaten and robbed. Let us imagine for a moment that we are in this position, we may feel like we have been run over by a truck. We are slipping in and out of consciousness as we hear the approach and the passing by of the priest and the Levite, as we wait in expectation that they will respond because our need and because of their beliefs. However, they move on without so much of a side-glance. Through our feelings of pain, we recognise that it matters little that they have valid excuses for doing so, and whether their reasons can be excused or justified. Placed in the position of the wounded, we hear the approach of the Samaritan from whom – as a Jew – we can expect nothing. But, to our astonishment, the Samaritan is seized with compassion and renders help.

We usually think of the 'Good Samaritan' in this parable as the Jesus-like figure, and indeed so he is for he went about doing good. But in a profounder sense, the man who fell among thieves is the representative of Jesus – the neighbour who needs our help. It is Jesus who is the one who is stripped and beaten and left half dead that the Samaritan takes care of. This is the heart of the Christian gospel because as Jesus claimed, 'by doing it to the least of these among you, you do it to me'.

The message of this parable can be described as the theology of the 'Corporate Son of Man', which is that we find Jesus in everyone we meet. Because the Christ spirit is the representative of all humankind and is present in every living person, therefore anyone can be a Jesus representative whether they know it or not and to receive them is to receive the sacred spirit of God. As Michael Morwood said in an address to the Progressive Christian Network of Victoria, 'If you want evidence of God working in the world, think today on your own actions; did you feed your children, did you help your neighbour, did you visit someone who was sick or alone? These are the acts of the God Spirit!'

The person we help confers on us a favour because they make Jesus real to us, they allow us to touch, handle and serve the sacred Spirit of Jesus. Clearly the metaphorical message of this story is that here is someone showing the compassion of God whom the Jews would least expect it from. Here is evidence of God's reign revealed in the most unlikely circumstance. All we believe about God is being turned upside down, because it means that our values and preconceived opinions are being radically challenged.

Hence the gospel call to us is to reach out to those in need: not because we think that is what God wants us to do; not because we will get a big tick in God's special book – you know the one that records 'who has been naughty or nice'. Not because we may convert this person to Christianity and add to the coffers of the church. But simply because they need us and by reaching out in this way, Jesus the human one will be revealed to us, and we will glimpse something of the reality of God and then maybe, just maybe, it will convert our thinking from a negative God image to a positive one.

Let us not ask the question, 'Who is my neighbour'? But let us ask the question, 'To who am I a neighbour'? Who is it that I can reach out to and embrace, to whom can I show mercy in the name of a compassionate God? This is the very heart of the gospel.

In John 15:12ff, we read that Jesus said, 'This is my commandment, that you love one another as I have loved you. No one has greater love than this, to lay down one's life for one's friends'. We also read in John 15:15ff that Jesus loved his friends such as Lazarus and his disciples when he told them, 'I do not call you servants any longer, because the servant doesn't know what the master is doing; but I have called you friends, because I have made known to you everything that I have heard from my Father'. So Jesus, through his love of his friends, not only shared openly his wisdom, but included them as companions and equals, which made them feel worthwhile, accepted and needed.

The second story on Jesus' reaction to racism is recorded in the story of the Syrophoenician woman. Let us now quickly recap the story. Jesus has left Galilee with his disciples; he is taking a holiday and has decided to go to the regional towns of Tyre and Sidon. He would not be as well known to the non-Jews there, so here is a chance for him to take a break because people will not recognise him. According to Mark's Gospel, he wanted to be alone with his disciples. Suddenly out of left field this woman recognises him as Jesus who is a healer, and one who can cast out demons. This woman has a child who is uncontrollable as a result of demonic possession, and must be locked up in her house.

To get Jesus' attention she shouts at him. She first refers to him as 'Sir' but later calls him 'Son of David'. This is not a term of endearment, as one would expect; but it is a racist slur. She is actually calling him a Jew. In the vernacular of the day, she is saying 'Hey you, Jew boy'. She is describing him by his race. How do you think Jesus would be feeling at this point? Here he is having a break from the demands of his ministry, and suddenly he is recognised by a woman who racially calls him a Jew.

What does Jesus do? He responds, as most of us would do in a hostile environment because he simply ignores her. He continues to walk away because it is degrading to be singled out in this way. But the woman is persistent; she doesn't give up and follows him so that there is a further embarrassment, so much so that the disciples urge him to respond, 'You have to do something because this woman is just making a scene'.

You can imagine Jesus saying, 'Why should I respond to her? She is a racist. Why should I respond to a non-Jew?' Eventually, Jesus does stop and the woman comes to him with a significant change in attitude – she falls at his feet and pleads for him to help her. The cry is 'Please help me'. Then Jesus utters the words we would normally not associate with him, 'It is not fair to take the children's food and throw it to the dogs'. Now, perhaps, we need some explanation of these words. It is not 'give' to the dogs but to 'throw' or cast off. It is dismissive, but now comes the telling part –the word 'dog' when translated literally means a female dog, or as we would say today 'bitch'.

So what did Jesus really mean? Was he annoyed that this woman had made a racist comment? We all know that racial slurs can hurt deeply, and if she wanted his help, then this vibrant, outgoing, Gentile woman had played the wrong card.

Although we cannot gauge the exact tone, my interpretation is that the first response by Jesus is saying 'Mind your language', 'Are you aware of what you are saying?' Was he also saying, 'Act responsibly!'? Certainly, the woman must have picked up that she overstepped the mark of sensitive dialogue by her actions, and so she changes the tone of her voice and her choice of words. Jesus' confronting language was perhaps a trigger to say, 'You have overstepped the mark of decency'. This woman had drawn a boundary based on race and she had divided society into Jews and Gentiles.

Jesus takes her on in a verbal stoush and confronts her with her own negativity and insensitivity. She accepts his admonishment and one could guess, with an almost cheeky smile, she responds with, 'Yes, Lord, but even the dogs get the crumbs from the masters table'. This is a great comeback, because without actually saying so she is admitting that she has stepped over the line.

Hence the response from Jesus, and you can almost see his smile, 'Woman, great is your faith. Let it be done for you as you wish.'

The message here is clear and it is this; racism and name calling show a lack of respect for each person, regardless of race, creed, or sexual orientation and must be replaced by God's realm where all are welcomed and the cry of 'Jew', 'White Trash', or any other derogatory term is no longer tolerated in God's kingdom.

It is up to us to ensure that in the name of God we do not tolerate this sort of behaviour in others. In the name of God, we must challenge it whenever it raises its ugly head. When Jesus arrived in Jerusalem he almost immediately confronts opposition to his teaching. Mark's account of this situation is different from Luke's because Luke adds the parable of the 'Good Samaritan' by way of illustrating the point about loving God and loving one's neighbour. This is one of the most significant parabolic teachings of Jesus.

Mark, in contrast to Luke, summarises the conflict with the scholars by condensing the whole of the Jewish law into two brief commandments. The first commandment is the traditional Jewish *Shema* which we find in Deuteronomy 6:4-5, 'Hear, O Israel, the Lord is our God, the Lord alone. You shall love the Lord your God, with all your heart, and with all your soul, and with all your might'. This quotation from Deuteronomy favourably shows how much this statement of Jewish law is in parallel with Jesus' teaching.

It is often said that while there may be many faiths, there is only one humanity, so while we may experience the sacred source differently we are bound together by our humanity. Jesus reinforces the importance of our love for each other when he states what has become known as the 'Golden Rule' – 'You shall love your neighbour as yourself' (Mark 12:31), it is also quoted in Matthew 22:39.

Now Jesus wasn't the first person to make such a quote. In fact, similar wisdom sayings can be found in most of the major religions. We read in Leviticus 19:18 'But you should love your neighbour as yourself'. In this context, the commandment has the effect of countering vengeance in one's family or tribe. In Judaism, the Pharisee Hillel was once asked by a student to teach him about the Torah, standing on one leg. Quite a brave request when one realises that there are more than 600 laws in the Torah. Fortunately for the student, Hillel replies: 'What you find hateful do not do to another. This is the whole of the law, everything else is commentary. Now go and learn that'.

In the sixth century BCE, it was Confucius who said, 'Never do unto others what you would not like them to do to you'. And Buddha who was born in the second century BCE has also made a similar comment when he advises, 'Consider others as yourself'.

What is intriguing about this text is that Jesus is quoting the most important words in the Hebrew Bible; 'Hear, O Israel, the Lord our God is one Lord'. This text is known by its first word, the imperative *'Shema'*. For the observant Jew, this pledge of allegiance to the one God is the first prayer to be said on waking, and the final prayer before falling asleep. It is the first prayer that a Jewish child is taught, and it is the last words a Jew says before death.

Down through the ages, for the Jew, the Shema is the ultimate cry of faith. It was with *Shema* on their lips that the Jewish martyrs were tied to the inquisitor's stake and when they entered the Nazi gas chambers.

Jews hold the Book of Deuteronomy in high regard because it is an educational text and the *Shema* needs to be taught. The form of education commended by Deuteronomy is nurture, and nurture is about feeling a sense of belonging. Education and nurture is not the same. All nurture is education, but not all education is nurture and nor should it be.

Nurture as advocated by Deuteronomy is certainly 'learning about' and 'learning from', but above all it is 'learning within'. The child is brought up within the community of faith and in the early years the community is the family home. Nurture takes place at home where the faith by which the family lives is seen as a natural discussion point.

This text indicates to us that Jesus knew and loved Deuteronomy and was familiar with the *Shema*. His insight is to bring the text from Deuteronomy together with the injunction from Leviticus, that we are called to love our neighbours as ourselves. Thus Deuteronomy is a profoundly important educational manifesto because there is a tenderness to much of its teaching, for example in Deuteronomy 24:10-22 we read about the importance of compassion for the poor.

When Jesus is confronted with the world of flesh, evil and painful death, he is armed with the *Shema* and the commandment he derives from Leviticus. We have some understanding of what these texts meant for Jesus and how he maintained the moral coherency of his belief, even when faced with his own demons, but how does this help us?

Do we as individuals, as a community of faith and as a nation reflect the 'nurture' expressed in this wonderful text? And if not why not? Our current response to asylum seekers and refugees should give us a great cause for concern as people of faith.

Perhaps the greatest concern of all is the apathy shown, not only by our political leaders, but also by the general public in redressing this situation. The Chief of Amnesty International in the 90s, Irene Khan, pointed out that she had worked in Australia in the eighties and was proud of this country's achievements in upholding international law and the development of multiculturalism. So what has happened over the last decade or so? And do we want to be different than we are now?

Or are we comfortable about who we are at this time? Does Jesus who calls us to follow these two commandments, make us just a little uncomfortable about the way we are demonstrating our so-called Christian beliefs? Are we as Christians ensuring that we are communicating to our impressionable young the compassion that Jesus finds in Deuteronomy and Leviticus? Most importantly are we educating our children with nurture? If we aren't, what can we do to reverse this situation?

In the article by Andrew Hamilton in the on-line magazine *Eureka Street*, in July 2019, he asks the question, 'Whatever Happened to Kindness to Strangers?' Hamilton draws a comparison with our current brutal attitude to asylum seekers, refugees and immigrants to that of our generous and compassionate attitude to strangers from other countries after the Second World War. At that time, world leaders were seeking to base international relations on cooperative approach by sharing the burdens of support and care for these people. They recognised the disastrous consequences of xenophobic nationalism and the role that inequality has in breeding it, as displayed by our current government's policy of 'Operation Sovereign Borders'. The world leaders in the 1940s supported the need for a just and cooperative international order, which was rule-based and met the needs of those who were disadvantaged in most part through no fault of their own.

The post-war vision of a better world order enshrined a 'hospitality to strangers' which saw in them 'possibilities' instead of 'threats', so that they included them with embrace, rather than excluded them which encouraged relationships to grow with these refugees instead of codifying and limiting them.

As Hamilton concludes in his article: 'Suspicion breeds fear; fear generates hostility, and hostility breeds even more suspicion'. An example of suspicion breeding fear can be found in the those young Australian Nationals who adopted a position of neo-Nazi politics which arose primarily out of suspicion and fear of strangers.

In the name of Jesus of Nazareth, may God grab us by the collar and shake us out of our apathy!!!! In the name of Jesus, we must endorse and live out the 'Golden Rule' while there is still hope. I firmly believe that one day Australia will again stand tall as a nation known for its compassion and understanding, particularly for those who have been marginalised and abused and who are seeking safety in our country, but to do so we must be prepared not only to adopt but to embrace the values of Jesus of Nazareth.

If we do this, I believe we will become a nation that will no longer cage children seeking refuge and embrace, behind razor wire. We will become an Australia that will protect the rights of all its citizens and ensure that the rule of law which claims all people are innocent until proven guilty is the inalienable right of all. It will be a nation that reaches out with a compassionate embrace to strangers.

We will be an Australia that will refuse to be engaged in the occupation and armed conflict of a country, primarily for diplomatic reasons. We will also be a nation that refuses to participate in a conflict that increasingly contributes to the deaths of innocent people. I believe that, in the future, Australia will raise up leaders who will speak honestly, and freely admit their mistakes. Today, our task as friends of Jesus is to commit ourselves to embracing our God and as Jesus encourages us, reach out to others with compassion.

And by our example we will nurture our children, so that they will be the change our society desperately requires if we are to embrace the message of the Golden Rule as spoken by Jesus, which states: 'You are to love the Lord your God with all your heart and all your soul and all your mind and with all your energy'. The second is this: 'You are to love your neighbour as yourself'.

Jesus' values and the role of women, and in particular the influence of his mother Mary, are of vital importance in shaping the personality of this Galilean sage. According to Luke, women travelled with Jesus and his male disciples and were a significant part of his teaching and preaching. It is important to realise that in the first century it would have been quite unusual to support the equality of women. It appears then that Jesus saw women as being equal to men and this is emphasised by the fact that these women are recognised as 'enthusiastic followers' travelling the countryside in mixed company.

What influenced Jesus to accept women as equal? My good friend and colleague the late Rev. Dr John Bodycomb shared with me his understanding which is that as mothers play a significant role in the development of values in children, it very possible that Jesus' mother Mary taught him about gender equality.

It is also considered that Mary would have played a significant role in the development of Jesus' feminine side. Chris Geraghty, has recently confirmed this in his challenging book *Jesus the Forgotten Feminist* where he traces through the scriptures how Jesus practised a radically inclusive approach to women, which challenged the beliefs and practices of his culture and his community.

In western culture, it has only been in the last 30 to 40 years that men have been consciously learning to be sensitive to the needs of women by recognising the feminine side of their own personalities, such as tenderness, sensitivity, empathy and compassion. Thirty years ago these men were referred to as SNAGS which, suggested that they were 'sensitive new age guys'.

A second reason to honour Mary is for the shaping of Jesus' piety; his faith and how he thought about God. Some of my own research has thrown light on this. John Bodycomb's own research in this matter of a large sample of church goers regarding the influence of mothers on the development of the values in their children revealed that 47% nominated their mother as the person who most influenced their religious beliefs and only 12% nominated their father. My own experience is that my egalitarian values and my commitment to democratic socialist ideals are a direct result of my mother's influence, not only by what she said but how she personally responded to the needs of others.

This difference between the influence of mothers and fathers lends weight to that observation by Sir James Barrie, author of *Peter Pan*, when he wrote, 'The God to whom little boys say their prayers has a face very like their mother's.'

Those who have read John Bodycomb's book *Gordon Powell Reflects* may recall that the Rev. Gordon Powell told him that the greatest influence of all on him was his mother

Louisa – not just by reading Bible stories to him and his little brother, but by her whole life and faith. She also exercised the mother's prerogative of chiding him when she thought this was warranted. Gordon said, 'One day, I suggested changing something I had promised to do', and she said 'You must always keep faith with your public'. On another occasion, Gordon had posted up a list of rather good exam results on the family notice board outside the family kitchen. As Gordon said, his mother gently chided me and said, 'Isn't that blowing your own trumpet a bit?"

A third reason to honour Mary is for the shaping of Jesus' priorities. You will remember that Luke, the gospel writer, has Jesus getting up in the Nazareth synagogue and reading a passage from Isaiah that is all about the overcoming of poverty, captivity, disability and oppression – the great obstacles to human freedom and fulfilment.

And then Jesus says in effect, 'These will be the priorities in my ministry'. But where is the evidence to support that these values of Jesus came from Mary? For the clue to this connection, we need to go back a little in Luke's Gospel. This evidence is found in the song of Mary, which we call the 'Magnificat'. The following is an interpretation of the first eight verses by the Rev. Dr John Bodycomb written in an unpublished manuscript titled *Heretics Ablaze*.

> My heart is overflowing with praise of my Lord. My soul is full of joy in God my Saviour, for he has specially noted me, his humble servant, and after this all the people who shall ever be will call me the happiest of women! The One who can do

all things has done great things for me – Oh, holy is his name!

Truly, his mercy rests on those who fear him in every generation. He has shown the strength of his arm, he has swept away the high and mighty. He has set kings down from their thrones and lifted up the humble. He has satisfied the hungry with good things, and sent the rich away with empty hands...

In his book *The Jesus Creed*, Scot McKnight claims the Magnificat contains virtually every theme in Jesus' teaching and ministry. He says, 'I think she sang him to sleep with these kinds of songs.' Be that as it may, I am suggesting it is high time we honoured Mary for the way she shaped Jesus' personality, his piety and his priorities. We must make sure that we pay tribute to Mary's nurturing of Jesus and the encouragement she would have given him to put into practice the values she imparted to him. Mary is a vital part of the Jesus story so we must make sure her great contribution to his development is appropriately recognised.

So why did people create these stories about Jesus as saviour and king? Why did they embellish the stories about Jesus so as to make them almost impossible to believe? Was it to draw a connection between God and Jesus? Did the gospel writers want to establish evidence that Jesus was divine by attributing to him miraculous acts? The stories of Jesus may possibly be a reflection of the regard that people had for him rather than factual details. However we interpret this, it does indicate that this wisdom sage from Nazareth had a profound impact on the people he met and developed relationships with.

How close was the personal relationship between Jesus and his friends and disciples? In Matthew 12:46, we read the following dialogue, while Jesus is speaking to the crowds with his disciples while his mother and brothers were standing outside but were wanting to speak with him. As a result, someone came to Jesus and told him this. Jesus replied, 'Who is my mother and who are my brothers?' And pointing to his disciples, he said, 'Here are my mother and brothers! For whoever does the will of my Father in heaven is my brother, sister and mother'. This response explains to us about the closeness of the relationship between Jesus and his disciples as he describes it as one of an 'extended family'. Here we see Jesus in a kindred relationship with those close to him.

So what is it about Jesus that influences people? Is it his words and actions? The Jesus Seminar scholars, in analysing the 'Voiceprint' of Jesus and placing these words in their historical matrix, have given us a glimpse of the influence of this historical figure. I would also add that people were attracted to Jesus because he made them feel worthwhile and valued. He conveyed a passion about life that was empowering. He was also able to convey that he understood how people felt when they were devalued, or when they were excluded from community as a result of the mores and laws associated with normal bodily functions, which declared them as being 'unclean' and in turn unworthy to be embraced.

The following is a summary of the writings of Lloyd Geering because they parallel other writers associated with the Westar Institute such as Borg, Crossan, and Funk in particular. These scholars have examined the gospels in great detail in an attempt to find the credible or authentic voiceprint of Jesus. The conclusion that these scholars came to after an extensive and scholarly examination is that the Jesus of the gospels is not the Jesus of Christian orthodoxy. Many of the claims of Jesus as presented in the gospels had been added by the gospel writers in many cases to respond to the needs of the faith community of that day. In summary, many of the claims attributed to Jesus' divinity were not the words of Jesus himself, but came from the fertile minds of the gospel writers.

From Geering's viewpoint, when we strip away the overlay of the gospel writers we discover that Jesus spoke in aphorisms (one liners) and parables. Thus Jesus comes from the sagely tradition of holy people and probably the closest other sagely writer is Ecclesiasticus. It was Ecclesiasticus who said, 'Good things and bad, life and death, poverty and wealth all come from God'. In a similar way, Jesus said, 'God causes the sun to rise on the bad and the good and sends rain on the just and the unjust'. Jesus spoke of sparrows and lilies of the field because, for sages the reverence for God was a reverence of nature. Jesus spoke of everyday matters and in so doing, he made secular or 'this worldly' statements. He talked about the need to care for each other and how divisiveness brings about hurt in personal relationships.

There is a closeness between Ecclesiasticus and Jesus because both deal with issues that are common to all humans regardless of their cultural differences. However, Jesus – in the quality and depth of his teaching – took this unconventional wisdom to a new level.

Jesus taught people to look to the future with hope and faith, but he never encouraged people to let God take over their lives and their decisions, as do many modern right wing evangelists. Like the sages before him, he urged people to take responsibility for their own lives. He encouraged people to also take responsibility for their own actions and to work for the common good. Jesus spoke much more about how to live wisely and act righteously than he did about what to believe about God.

It was St Augustine who turned the 'action orientation' or 'right action' into 'right belief' which is a belief that Jesus' death brought forgiveness. This led to the beginning the doctrine of 'Atonement'.

Jesus used the term the 'kingdom of God' to refer to the ideal way of ordering human society. He said that the kingdom of God would come quietly and unobtrusively. In reality, he claimed that the kingdom of God had already come, as referred to earlier. He likened the kingdom to heaven; unlike the kingdoms of the world, the kingdom of God spread from the bottom, as people developed self-discipline and mutual concern for one another. In the kingdom of God, people were to get the best out of life for themselves and for others.

An often neglected attribute of Jesus is his humour as found in such statements as: 'Again I tell you it is easier for a camel to go through the eye of a needle than for someone who is rich to enter the kingdom of God' (Matthew 19:24).

And 'If anyone wants to sue you and take your coat, give your cloak as well' (Matthew 5:40). In Jesus' day, a person only wore two garments, so to give both would mean that the person would walk from the court naked.

The instruction to love your enemies in Luke 6:27 – 'Love your enemies, do good to those who hate you, bless those who curse you, pray for those who abuse you' – is a revolutionary and unique teaching of Jesus. Jesus, by his comments, was able to arouse antagonism with both scholars and capitalists alike. His teachings were so outrageous that some questioned his sanity. His preaching of an alternative kingdom aroused the concern of Roman authorities.

It is interesting to note that Paul, a man who never met Jesus, began to provide the raw material for the creeds.

This understanding of the historical Jesus call us to ask the question, does church orthodoxy truly reflect the teaching and person of Jesus? In John Robinson's 1965 book *A New Reformation*, he raised the question of whether the church had become an archaic and well-protected institution for the preservation of something that is irrelevant and incredible. He also raised the question: 'Was real spiritual renewal occurring outside of the church and even in spite of it?'

The recovery of the voiceprints of the original Jesus has now opened up a middle way. As soon as we reflect on the original teachings of Jesus, we find the whole system of orthodox Christian doctrine and thought is disintegrating and that it is actually inconsistent with the teaching of Jesus. At times, it stands in moral condemnation.

The doctrine of the 'Atonement' is where Jesus dies for our sins because God requires moral justice. Today, our human sense of justice and compassion are morally offended by the idea that a loving God should sacrifice his son. Today, we are appalled at the very idea that any innocent person should be made to suffer for the wrongdoing of another.

Jesus himself denies the 'Atonement' in the parable of the 'Prodigal Son' which illustrates God as a forgiving and loving Father when he welcomes back his erring son. Jesus thus condemns Christian orthodoxy.

The church is not the kingdom! Jesus had no intention of founding a church and he never claimed to be God's only son, the Messiah. The institution of the church as a structure of power deserves to die as it has been doing for the last 300 years. We can still enter into a relationship with the authentic Jesus, but to do so it may require us to be more perceptive about human frailty than society is currently facing. If we are to take this approach it will also require our theological institutions to change significantly their current teaching methods.

In summary then, the message of Jesus is, in the words of Bishop Shelby Spong, 'Go into the world and become involved, reach out to each other in love and seek out evidence of the spiritual energy we know as God in every circumstance, in every person. And wherever you find it, in whatever situation affirm it with all the power you can muster. Do not place conditions on it, but celebrate its beauty and live your life abundantly, loving wastefully and empowering each other to be all that you can be'. (This quotation comes from an article by Bishop Spong on the website of 'Progressing Spirit'.)

Chapter 4
The Values of Friendship

THE VALUES OF FRIENDSHIP are defined by the amount of energy invested in any element of friendship. The values we hold are the measure of the intensity of our friendships. When we speak of placing a high value upon a particular idea or feeling we are expressing that this idea or feeling exerts a considerable force in instigating and directing our behaviour. For example, a person who values 'honesty' will expend a great deal of questioning energy in search for it. Conversely, if something is considered to be of trivial value, it will have little energy attached to it.

The absolute energy value of a feeling cannot be measured because it is so personal and individual. One simple, but not necessarily accurate, way of determining the energy level of a value is to directly ask a person what his or her priorities are. For example, does 'truth' have greater energy for you than 'respect'?

Values will also initiate bodily reactions; for example, some people may become physically emotional if they believe they are being treated unjustly. This may cause the heart to beat faster and the breathing to become faster and deeper. All of these responses indicate that the issue of justice for this person has a high-energy value.

If values are repressed into the 'shadow side' of personality, then the energy will appear elsewhere in the 'persona' at the expense of the positive side of personality. Satisfying the ego at the expense of facing the reality of the energy of values can be the enemy of positive friendships.

Do a person's needs operate always in the service of some value and are all behaviours determined by values? If they are, it clearly means that to understand any behaviour we must be aware of the person's strongly held values. Hence the values we hold are critical to the way we behave, because they not only affect our physical wellbeing, they will also impact on our interpersonal affectation and transcendental activities such as our personal philosophy and spiritual understanding.

According to social psychologists, many life conditions are determined by early external forces such as the feeling of security in the womb or the enjoyment and satisfaction of receiving comforting interaction through feeding from the mother's breast. Socialising with others in the nursery also has an impact on being accepted and loved. All of these experiences will have an impact on determining the values that a person holds. Interaction with our environment, even at this early age, will fashion the values that we hold; hence the vital importance of good nurturing.

Values not only develop through the person's image of themselves as a result of the interaction with their environment. Values can also be adopted from others and perceived as being the result of their own personal experience. Friends of Jesus may have adopted and embraced his values, although they may not have experienced them directly.

For a healthy integrated adjustment to our personal environment we need to continuously evaluate our life experiences in the light of the values we hold. An important value is the willingness to accept the possibility of change and to modify our behaviour accordingly. Any fixed value has the danger of preventing a person from reacting positively to new experiences. Flexibility is crucial in adjusting to life changing conditions. The term 'progressive' can be defined, first, as an adjective; it simply means something that develops gradually or in separate stages. As a noun, it is defined as a person implementing social reform or new liberal ideas. A progressive Christian then can be defined as a person introducing or promoting change gradually or in stages.

So what are the values that underpin and influence positive growth-promoting friendships?

For me, the most crucial value in the development of friendships is the value of 'compassion'. The Collins Dictionary definition of the word 'compassion' as a noun comes from the late Latin *compassio* or fellow-feeling and from *cum pati*, to suffer with. Hence, compassion is: 'a feeling of distress and pity for the suffering and misfortune of another, often including the desire to alleviate it'.

The word 'compassion' in Hebrew (as well as in Aramaic), is usually translated in the plural form of the noun. In its singular form, however, the word means 'womb'. In the Hebrew Bible, compassion is both a feeling and a way of being that flows out of one's sense of compassion. It is frequently linked to its association with womb: a woman feels compassion for the child of her own womb; a man feels compassion for his brother, who comes from the same womb.

For Marcus Borg (1989), compassion is a spiritual shift and is a result of some pretty hard work for most of us. According to Marcus Borg, there are four different types of compassion which he describes as reflective (thinking), emotional (feeling), active (doing), and contemplative (experiencing). While our goal, according to Borg, is to integrate all four of these at some point, he admits that this is a challenge. As he explains, we are called as followers of Jesus to show compassion (love, as a mother loves her unborn child). I think this means you may not know your child, who she or he is going to be, but you still 'love' or feel compassion for them.

My suggestion is that you at least can love or have compassion for the kinds of people you describe, but it might be limited to a thinking type if that is the best you can do. You could take the time to wonder what kind of childhood they had and what kind of an early life they had to endure.

Compassion is the primary virtue in shaping the relationships we have with each other because it involves inclusiveness and inclusive caring especially in close-knit families and communities. Justice is the social systemic form of compassion and it is compassion that changes the world, because to respond to another person out of love is the demonstration of our most valued response.

Compassion can sometimes lead to intimacy. The term intimacy involves a 'mutually consensual relationship where two individuals reciprocate feelings of trust by sharing their deepest feelings and concerns'. A true understanding of intimacy is not just about two bodies merging for sex but about the deepening of the relationship through mutual trust and the sharing of their deepest emotions. Intimacy occurs only when the person feels safe knowing that the information and the emotional reactions they are sharing will remain confidential.

The second important value underpinning the elements of friendship is integrity. The definition of 'integrity' that I am using is an 'adherence to moral and ethical principles, which provides a wholeness of moral character'. A person of integrity is 'morally coherent' which means that the ethical principles they hold in one situation will be held in other similar situations. Hence, their friends can always anticipate their personal views.

I personally use the method of 'Moral Coherency' to examine my own integrity taught to me by Professor Wolf Wolfensberger from Syracuse University's Training Institute for Human Service Planning who I studied under in 1990. Professor Wolfensberger's method was to encourage human service workers to consistently reflect on the personal values they held to ensure that their words, actions and beliefs were congruent. As a result, I continue to regularly reflect on my own moral coherency. I do this primarily to raise to consciousness my unconscious rejection of others. Often the reason for my rejection of others and their attitudes lies primarily with the influence of my personally ego-centred needs. It is by reflecting that I can examine these personality forces and place them in a more realistic perspective. This is an important activity because many people, including those with disabilities, are often victimised by the language used to describe their situation.

An example of moral coherent thinking is if my values regarding the 'sanctity of life' are to be coherent, I cannot support 'capital punishment'. Hence, if I condemn the brutal murder of a person, I cannot call for the murderer to be killed by the State.

There is value in spending time on reflective/meditation to ensure that the values we hold are being consistently revealed in our words and actions. In doing so, we will become morally coherent. Our friends will then accept that it is our integrity that determines who we are as a person. At the very least, those close to us will know they are engaging with a real person.

The third value which is vital in any friendship is empathy. Empathy can be defined as the ability to sense a person's private inner world as if it were your own, without losing this 'as if' quality. Empathy is essential in understanding how a person is feeling in any particular situation so it is vital in any positive growth-promoting relationship.

Therefore, empathy is not just understanding the words, but being able to experience the feelings be they confusion, anger, fear of the unknown or the feelings of happiness, affection and love. To truly place yourself in the position to understand the feelings of another can at times cause personal anxiety, because if we truly open ourselves to the feelings of another human being, we risk the possibility of needing to make changes in the way we behave as a friend.

The value of empathy is in conveying to another that their feelings are real and in some cases justified and that they may require support and comfort. Achieving complete empathy is an almost impossible task but the attempt to understand feelings will convey that you are trying to understand the feelings and this in itself is a bonding activity.

By conveying our desire to understand more fully what our friend is experiencing conveys a positive regard for that person. This regard must be conveyed as 'unconditional' to be truly effective, because 'unconditional regard' does not carry with it a judgmental attitude.

A good friend once referred to my attitude to friendship as something akin to that of a small, pampered puppy dog who runs up to all people expecting to be loved and welcomed and never expecting to be rejected. Even when the dog is rejected to the point of a smack on the nose, it still comes back, thinking this is part of a game and not for real.

The importance of unconditional regard is that it has the power to encourage those who receive it to offer it to others. Having been raised by a loving mother and six loving sisters, I had difficulty in believing that people would not see me as loveable. This could be the reason my friend characterised me as a 'pampered puppy'.

Love for each other must show unconditional positive regard, which means paying attention to friends regardless of how good or bad the behaviour is because your friendship requires you to attend to the total person. This certainly does not infer that certain behaviour cannot be challenged because if it is not, the continuing friendship will suffer.

The fourth value underpinning the elements of friendship is 'perseverance', which I have defined as the: 'persistence and tenacity underlining the attitude to not give up even in the face of great difficulties'. This value is extremely important when your relationship with a close friend is experiencing difficulties. Hanging in there with the aim of resolving conflicting issues is vital in the development of a relationship. Perseverance will also include the value of loyalty and loyalty can only be given when one shows consistency of thought, word and deed. Loyalty requires 'moral coherency'.

The fifth value is humility, which can be described as the quality or condition of being humble. In any relationship it is important to be aware of one's own strengths and weaknesses and to be grateful for the opportunity to have friendships. Displaying humility by being grateful reflects a modest estimate of one's self.

In my teens when I was playing Australian Rules football, I remember taking three marks over my opponent in the first fifteen minutes of the game. After taking the third mark, I held the ball in my opponent's face and said, 'This is what it looks like'. My opponent snarled back at me and said, 'You love yourself!' To which I replied, 'Yes I do because I am loveable'. In the second quarter of the game after some very sound physical thumpings from my opponent, I thought to myself, 'perhaps a tad of humility wouldn't have been out of place'. So humility in certain situations can even save you from a bruising.

Humility also encourages an attitude of 'altruism', which is a willingness to do things that would bring advantages to others even if it results in disadvantages for you.

Of course, there are many values not mentioned above which will affect the quality of friendships and each of us will need to embrace those values that give us the energy to maintain positive growth-promoting friendships. I believe that the values mentioned here are most essential for this to occur.

The values that have been outlined above must be underpinned by a philosophy that emphasises a congenial regard for others. Unless the primary element in our value system is the true worth of the individual, we are unlikely to experience a sense of real caring or a desire to understand the needs of the other. It is also important to recognise that positive values also show a respect for ourselves and this will allow us to truly realise our human potential. Relationships that value us as worthwhile human beings bring us to a sense of wholeness.

Further, I strongly believe that if the world were governed by the values that good friends share, then there would be world peace and a significant decrease in the social evils we face in our society.

Chapter 5

Where Do Our Values Originate?

IF VALUES PROVIDE THE FOUNDATION for the way people live and respond to their world, then it is important to understand how these values have been developed. So what is it that influences and shapes the choice of the values we hold?

As demonstrated in the last chapter, it is our personal values that influence and shape our choice and quality of interpersonal relationships. Do we choose our values or are they simply adopted by us because of our early childhood experiences? What influences do formal education, peer groups and media play in the shaping of values? Most social psychologists agree that the primary values a person internalises in childhood will remain with them into adulthood. As we grow to maturity there will be other influences, such as those mentioned above, that will cause us to challenge and at times modify the values we internalised in our early years.

When we are confronted with new life experiences – be it at school or work, social activities or personal relationships – we may question the values that were instilled in us by our parents. Questions will arise such as what did my parents mean about being open, honest and caring. How do these values in my competitive world help me to achieve success, promotion, or wealth? For example as a sales representative, merchant banker or stockbroker, will I hold different values to those of a medical practitioner, social worker or teacher?

This all boils down to whether the values I hold truly reflect the person I understand myself to be. Do the values I hold allow me to be morally coherent? To understand the impact of personal values on the broader society, we need first of all to understand how these values have been shaped. Are they the result of convenience or are they things I believe are integral for me and right for all those people I relate to?

Let us now explore more fully the influences of family, education, peers, social affiliations, such as social and sporting clubs, as well as public and social media.

In examining the important early childhood influence of parents and family on values development, we need first to explore the early influence of attachment and bonding with parents. Attachment occurs at a very early stage in our personal development and can be a powerful influence in the shaping of values.

Bowlby (1979) and Ainsworth (1978) define the term 'attachment' as, 'A deep and enduring emotional bond that connects one person to another across time and space'. They also state that attachment does not have to be reciprocal, so one person may have an attachment to another individual that is not shared. This will often occur between a pregnant mother and her unborn child.

Attachment is characterised by particular behaviour in children such as seeking closeness to the attachment figure, especially when upset or threatened i.e., the importance of cuddling. Most child psychologists agree that attachment is present in all cultures and this explains how the parent/child relationship emerges and impacts on subsequent development.

Bowlby's 'evolutionary' theory of attachment suggests that children are biologically pre-programmed to form attachments with others, because this is essential to surviving. According to John Bowlby, attachment is determined by the parent's attitude and behaviour towards the infant's needs. Secure attachment occurs when the caregiver is sensitive and consistent in responding to the child's needs. It follows that parents who reject or neglect the child's need for attention will lead to insecure attachment.

Further research, such as that conducted by psychologist Harry Harlow in the 1950s and 60s with young rhesus monkeys demonstrated that the key determinate of attachment is not food, as was original assumed, but 'care' and 'responsiveness'. His method was to take baby monkeys from their mothers and place them in isolation. They had no contact with each other or anyone else.

For periods of three months and up to nine months, he kept them in isolation. He then put them back in the company of other monkeys and observed their behaviour in an attempt to explore the impact of not forming an attachment. Harlow's observations showed that the monkeys that had been isolated began to display rather bizarre behaviour, such as clutching or hugging their bodies and rocking compulsively.

Harlow also observed that the previously isolated monkeys showed a fear of other monkeys and as a result of this fear they became aggressive towards them. The experimental group were unable to communicate or socialise with the others and they also engaged in self-mutilation. The longer they had been kept in isolation, the more extreme their behaviour.

A further experiment by Harlow was to separate eight monkeys from their mothers immediately after birth by placing them in cages with access to two surrogate mothers, one made of wire which had fitted to it a bottle of milk which allowed the monkeys to suckle. The second was made of cloth. These animals were studied for twenty- three weeks.

The results showed that all monkeys spend more time with the cloth mother, although she had no milk. Each monkey would go to the wire mother to get milk when hungry, but once satisfied, would return to the cloth mother for the rest of the day. If frightening objects were placed in the cage, the young monkeys would seek refuge with the cloth mother.

It was also discovered that a monkey in the cage with the cloth mother would be more adventurous in exploring their environment. This supported the evolutionary theory of attachment in that it is the sensitive response and security of the caregiver which is most important if positive attachment is to occur.

Harlow concluded that for a monkey to develop normally, it must have some interaction with an object to which they can cling especially in the first few months of life. As clinging is a natural response for monkeys, being able to cling decreases stress and provides comfort.

Harlow has been criticised for the emotional harm he caused these young monkeys and their mothers. However, his findings did support the work of Bowlby and Ainsworth.

Bowlby's studies also suggest that a child initially forms only one primary attachment and this attachment figure provides a secure base for exploring the world. The early attachment relationship acts as a prototype for all future social relationships so to disrupt this process in the early stage of life can have a significant consequence for the future.

My friend and colleague Rev. Dr John Bodycomb related to me a conversation he had some years ago with the well-known psychiatrist Dr Ainslie Mears. They were discussing the different personality attributes between men and women such as tenderness, sensitivity, empathy and compassion. Dr Mears said that women were programmed for empathy in a way that men were not. That is not to say that men cannot learn these so-called feminine characteristics, but it wasn't natural to them as it is in women. Dr Mears also said that 'Quite simply, since the dawn of our history, a woman had to know how her baby was feeling before it was old enough to be able to tell her.'

I have found in my own research into the bonding between fathers and children with disabilities for a master's thesis, that fathers do have the desire and empathy to nurture their children. This study 'Bonding Between Father's and Children with Intellectual Disabilities' was conducted in 1996 at Flinders University in South Australia. This research was conducted with the support of thirty-two fathers and included a series of questionnaires describing their daily contact with their child and a personal interview with seventeen of the participants. The information revealed clearly that strong bonding was developing.

This research clearly determined that fathers want to be personally involved with the care and nurturing of their child's development in a range of activities. These men agreed that the childcare role is not gender specific, but they also agreed that it was their partners who played the primary childcare role.

The seventeen who participated in the in-depth interview all showed a strong attachment to their child and a desire to personally nurture the child towards greater independence. From a 'family systems' analysis it has been determined by researchers that when the father shows acceptance of the child, it encourages all other members of the immediate and extended family to accept the child also.

The information provided by this research affirmed the importance of the father's role in child rearing. Social psychologists have also emphasised the importance of an attachment process, which occurs between a father and a newborn child. They have named this process 'engrossment'.

I have personally experienced this process with the birth of my three children because I recognised how totally fascinated I became with them in the early months of their life. I would sit and gaze at them for hours; it was like being captivated by a work of art or a thing of beauty. Arriving home from work late at night, I would go directly into the nursery and unwrap the sleeping child just to observe them. My wife was not really appreciative of this obsessive engrossment because she would then have the responsibility to try to get the child back to sleep.

I also became aware that even at the age of three months, each of the children would lock into eye contact, which for me was an indication that they were attempting to communicate. During these events I would smile and they would smile in return and then I would say, 'I love you' to affirm that they were precious and special. Bonding does occur for men before language development. Of course, the mother has a nine months start on fathers in the attachment process because she has the responsibility of nurturing the child with her own body.

My research into the bonding of fathers and children with disabilities was important in establishing that father's can assist in child rearing by bonding with the child very early in the child's life. This bonding does occur when the father is a sole supervisor in childcare as well as in times of play.

Unfortunately, at this time, the fathers in the study experienced a lack of professional support in dealing with the emotional trauma of fathering a child with a disability. Those interviewed – when discussing their emotional response to the birth of their child – broke down in tears, even though the birth had occurred some year's prior. The only support they did receive was from a loving partner, family and close friends.

In one situation, the father was the primary carer because he and his wife had agreed that as she was a professional earning good money, he would remain at home to care for their child. The professionals in the supportive health services caring for the child still refused to negotiate with the father and would always make contact with his wife to discuss care issues. Training with health care professionals including paediatricians, was – and I gather still is – required in recognising the nurturing capabilities of men.

The research also discovered that including fathers in the communication of the diagnosis of the child's disability was also vital. In the majority of the cases, 30 out of the 32, the paediatrician informed the mother without the father being present. These fathers recounted the trauma of receiving a phone call from their distressed partner needing support, comfort and assurance after learning of the child's disability.

In two situations only, a paediatrician asked the father to be present at the time of the disclosure. It was the same paediatrician in both cases, who not only gave emotional support to the mothers but embraced and actually wept with the fathers. Each father said that as a result of this support they realised the importance of bonding with their child at birth.

In a later conversation with a group of doctors who showed an interest in this research, I suggested that they should encourage all fathers not to wear cologne or deodorant and to embrace their child immediately after birth and hold the child close to their bare chest so the child can smell the natural father. Research tells us that our olfactory sense has the strongest memory. Health professionals need training to ensure that they recognise the need for the father's involvement in developing attachment, socialisation and emotional support for their children, and professionals must plan to make this possible.

In conclusion, this research discovered that the birth of a child with a disability has a significant impact on the father emotionally and will, if not recognised, affect his interaction with the child as well as the attachment process. Further, it became evident that most fathers desire to be involved in the nurture and development of their children, and in some situations require support and affirmation to do so.

As attachment studies have shown the lack of bonding with the father may influence the development of the child's value system. Studies of child development for both children with disabilities and those without have confirmed this issue.

What other factors influence the values we hold?

It is widely recognised that schools have a significant influence on the values, attitudes and personal qualities of young people. Most educational systems recognise that the development of positive values are most likely to be reinforced when there is a partnership between the teacher and the families. One survey found that in twice as many primary schools as secondary schools, values education had been influenced by parent/community pressure, and that they had used the involvement of parents to take values education forward.

I am sure most parents would have faced the issue of a child disagreeing with them on a particular matter because, their teacher had expressed a different point of view in the classroom.

The values each child holds can also be challenged by the child's peers, particularly when they become involved in activities, be they sporting or purely social activities. This can occur as early as when a child is attending a pre-school. Some studies have suggested that girls, even in pre-school, focus more on their role in giving, but were also more aware of what they could expect to receive from a good friend. Boys often came under the influences of bad friends, and became physically active and aggressive, whereas girls were more empathetic, by taking the other child's perspective.

Another challenge to family values can occur as a result of the child's exposure to public media such as television or computerised programs. In many cases the exposure to these programs needs to be carefully monitored.

In most formal education systems, teachers and educational managers believe they are charged with the responsibility of preparing children to accommodate and positively respond to life situations. The aim of which is to assist each child, to maximise its human potential. If the role of teachers and the education system is to positively promote moral, social, cultural and spiritual development in cooperation with each family, then they need to be trained accordingly.

There will be times when the values of the teacher may conflict with the values of the family and this may cause conflict for the child. However, it is not only the teachers in the education system that will influence personal values but also the friendships of fellow students.

In today's modern society with the advanced technological development of mobile phones and computers, parents face a new intrusion contesting the family values and it is that of 'social media'. A major concern for a number of parents is the influence social media will have on the values and mental health of their children because a number of young people have been harassed and bullied by their peers via this medium. In some situations, where there has been savage personal attacks on the young person, usually by their peers, it has brought the young person to the point of contemplating and in some situations actually committing suicide.

We all have a great need to be accepted for who we are and to be well regarded by our peers, especially in our teenage years. The lack of control over what is communicated through social media leaves many young people emotionally vulnerable. Research from the University of Alberta in Canada reports that 23% of all teenagers have been the subject of cyber bullying which takes the form of personal memoirs shared along with unedited personal videos. All of these communications are aimed at destroying the reputation of another person via blackmail.

Also, this form of cyber bullying may force a person to question their personal values, which have been formed by family, their educational experience and supportive friends. These experiences can lead to the point of deconstructing one's values about justice and the caring nature of friendships.

A particular negative impact of social media is to encourage people to form artificial bonds over actual personal friendships. This artificial bonding demeans the conventional use of the term friend, where people actually get to know each other and converse through face-to-face conversations where intimate bonds can be formed through the sharing of emotions and physical interaction.

Adolescence is a time to explore the world in which we live, preferably in the company of trusted friends but it also comes with great risks. Parents, friends, and teachers must protect children from negative outcomes by maintaining open communication based on sound positive values.

One of the greatest dangers we face personally is the danger of allowing our ego to control our values. Many human values are developed as part of our culture and upbringing; however, one of the most powerful internal influences in values development is our personal ego. I am interpreting the word ego not in a Freudian understanding of the word but in a colloquial sense as the 'unhealthy and irrational sense of self, where our own importance is always paramount'.

Our adoption of certain values may be the result of early childhood training; however, the embrace of values that lead to the denigration, abuse and marginalisation of others in many situations, find their roots in uncontrolled ego identification. It is the ego that reinforces the belief that you are the most important person and your needs must always come first. The outcome of this self-absorption is a result of being ego-centred and this prevents us from being rational, objective, and most of all empathetic to the rights and needs of others. The values I now hold have been influenced by people who hold values that are not ego-centered.

If as a society we desire to develop a greater consideration of each other and rid the world of the social evils that cause so much pain and heartache, we must be aware that the

Where Do Our Values Originate?

influence of an uncontrolled ego which, will often prevent us from displaying compassion. In his book *Ego is the Enemy*, Ric Holiday argues that the solutions to the problem of a self-absorbing ego are the values of humility, compassion, self-awareness, diligence, resilience and a willingness to embrace realism. These are the values that will counteract arrogance and self-centred ambition and in this way we will prevent the ego from its belief in our own individual importance.

If we can remove the ego as a prime motivating force, we will be left with a reality that will encourage us to embrace our real selves which includes the importance in recognising the value of others. A crucial impact in the removal of the self-centred ego is the ability to again listen to others. To do this effectively, we need to have times of being silent so that we can listen to others and our inner selves. It is interesting to realise that listen is an anagram of silent. Hence to listen well we need to remain silent.

Using the process of seeking solitude for self-reflection daily, I am now aware when my ego is controlling the values I wish to hold. It is through contemplation that I am trying to raise to conscious the Spirit of wisdom that is within me. I am seeking to discover if there is a morally coherent pattern between what I believe and how I act. Am I recognising the rights and values of others? This process works for me, but each of us needs to explore what would work for them.

A recent example of how ego can confuse appropriate responses to need was when the vice-President of the USA was justifying the increase of nuclear weapons in America. He claimed, 'Peace comes from strength'. Compassionate values will tell us that 'peace' will only come when all people believe they have received 'justice'.

I am aware that my ego is controlling me when:

> I have a lack of empathy and compassion for others.
>
> I realise that what matters to me is the only thing I need to be concerned about.
>
> I am super critical of others – which is my way of justifying that I know better than anyone else how to handle matters, because I am always right.
>
> I have stopped listening to the advice of those close to me because they will feel my lack of empathy first.
>
> I need to recognise and accept that I am not the most important person in the world.

Forming a relationship based on morally coherent values will ensure that these values will become a vital part of the person's personality and character. It is values that form the foundation of who we are because it is values that will influence the choices we make, the friendships we form, the employment we undertake. Values will also influence all the other social activities we engage in, including the knowledge of our 'transcendent/spiritual' self.

In all likelihood, the values that we internalised as a child will remain with us into adulthood. The values we reject are

Where Do Our Values Originate?

the values that no longer reveal the true self or support the path of life we have chosen. The crucial questions for each of us are: 'Are the values I have been raised with the values I am living with today?' 'Do these values bring to my life a sense of happiness, contentment and a connection with all of life?'

To answer these vital questions and to understand what our values hold for us, we must be prepared to deconstruct them by openly and honestly reviewing their importance in our life. To ask, 'Are these the values I hold or are they simply the values that have been given to me by my parents?'

Fulfilled people are those who have grown up with positive life-affirming values or who through a crisis of conscience have modified their values to meet their personal needs.

Chapter 6
Defining the Social Evils We are Experiencing

SOCIAL ANALYSTS both in Australia and internationally have for some time now been raising their concerns regarding the social issues that currently plague our world. So what are the major social evils confronting our world at this time?

This issue has been highlighted also by concerns about the numerous armed violence situations through foreign invasion and civil unrest, which continue unabated in many parts of the world and particularly in the Middle East. The corresponding problems such as people seeking refuge and asylum from this violence as well as requiring life saving medical assistance, along with the concerns of food shortages and homelessness. In 2017, the world humanitarian crisis was the worst since the end of the Second World War in 1945 with 20 million people in just four countries facing starvation. In Syria, 11 million people have fled their homes as the result of years of armed conflict.

Defining the Social Evils We are Experiencing

In 2017, more than 30 million people were displaced with more than 20 million fleeing from armed conflict.

How do we in Australia respond to this crisis, because not a week goes by without many other social issues affecting the good of the community are being brought to our attention. First, let us examine the much-publicised violence against women in our society.

For example, in a Melbourne city parkland in August 2018, we learnt of the rape and murder of a young woman while she was walking home from a night out. This is only one incident that highlights the issues of sexism and violence toward women. In the nation's capital, female senators have alerted us to the sexualised comments critical of women that have been made privately in the senate chamber by male senators; the verbal attacks on our first female Prime Minister is an example of this problem. These male senators are not providing a positive example for our future male generations. The Australian Bureau of Statistics of Personal Safety Findings reveals a major community concern. It has been revealed that one in five women over the age of 18 years have been stalked during their lifetime, and one in five women experience harassment within the workplace.

More frighteningly, over a twelve-month period, on average, a current or former partner kills one woman each week. These statistics have a wider implication when we realise that domestic and family violence is the principal cause of homelessness for women and their children and contributes significantly to high levels of psychological stress.

The problem of violence against women is much greater statistically among indigenous women who are thirty-five times more likely to be hospitalised for family violence, than the wider female population. The Australia- wide Royal Commission into institutional violence has also revealed that women with disabilities are not exempt from physical abuse whilst in care.

A study in July 2018 produced a report by case managers working with migrant women at 'Women's Safety Services South Australia'. This report revealed that approximately seventy-five percent of their clients were experiencing anxiety created by the insecurity of their current visa situation. This problem is exacerbated by the fact that many of these women are particularly vulnerable to their partners because, many of these males come from cultures that condone violence in the marriage situation. These women find themselves in a situation where they believe that they have no legal protection for themselves or their children when they take out a family violence application.

The headline in the *Melbourne Age* in bold type, 3 August 2018, states: '**THIS MUST STOP**'. This article by Miki Perkins recounts the death of four women; further, that in three cases where charges have been laid, the accused men were either husbands or partners. The writer also reports that 39 women had died violently in Australia so far that year and that an overwhelming majority of violent incidents and femicides were at the hands of men. Perkins concludes that, 'That we should be furious that women in our state are still getting strangled and killed by men who are supposed to love them'. I would also add the question 'Where is the public outrage?'

In a study conducted by 'The Victorian Health Promotion Foundation' (VicHealth) in 2011, it was determined that in Australia forty-one percent of women have experienced violence since the age of fifteen years. One in five women has experienced sexual violence and one in three has experienced physical violence also; and it must be recognised that violence against women in Australia costs $21.7 billion per year. The primary instigators of violence against women are male intimate partners or men who are known to them.

Jacqui Watt, chief executive officer of the N.T.V. (No To Violence) organisation, reported in June 2019 that while intervention strategies are vital, NTV wants to stop family violence before it starts, and this will require educating young boys about the importance of respecting females. She raises the issue of the importance of relationships because in Australia family violence contributes more to death, disability and illness in women aged 18 to 44 than any other risk factor. Watt claims that although family violence takes many forms, the most frequently used by men is due to the fact that they wish to exercise power and control over both women and children.

Social researchers have clearly defined that the major cause of male violence lies in the sanctioning of our cultural expectations and attitudes towards girls and women. From a very early age, boys are confronted daily with messages that girls are inferior to them, are not their equal and can be degraded, humiliated and abused. We witness this attitude in every day interactions modelled and reinforced primarily by adult males and particularly by those in authority.

It is also time for a massive cultural shift and this will only occur when the community as a whole declares that the denigration of women is no longer, and never has been, a blokey joke. It is the responsibility of every person and particularly males to call out this abuse, whenever it occurs, and confront the perpetrators.

The Christian church has not been a vanguard in insisting on the equal rights of women. Why is it that women were such a powerful influence in the early church when many were not notable in public life? A woman's role was to maintain the home and bear children and while this may have restricted them from public life, it gave them an opportunity to exercise their influence in the home. The early Jesus movement relied on the house church for their meetings. It was mostly women who gave instruction and were the early teachers of the faith.

In addition, the inclusive theology that saw women the equal of men within the Christian community established by Jesus and endorsed by Paul was appealing to independent, free thinking women. Of course when these activities threatened the position of men in the community, it caused conflict.

A further social evil that is creating real concern in Australia is the matter of 'economic inequality'. At a time when wages have not increased for the longest period on record and cost of living continues to increase, the gap between the rich and the poor has continued to grow. We also have a situation where company profits are at an all-time high and a government that is intent on reducing company taxes to create even greater profits. Evidence is also coming to light that a number of companies are actually paying their staff well below the award wages – a claim being put forward by employee support groups as an 'act of theft'. There are also recorded cases of employers refusing to make a contribution to the government-supported superannuation programs.

Economists vary in their explanations for the slump in labour share but most agree that the rise of 'superstar' information technology companies with a relatively small labour force, and the weakening of union power primarily due to the demonisation of union activity by the political right, have allowed corporations to amass ever increasing wealth at the expense of workers' wages.

In personal terms, this means that many people (e.g. in the banking sector) have not received a pay rise in ten years while bank profits are continuing to rise. This has left an increasing number of employees wondering if the employers will ever recognise the values of a 'fair and equitable distribution of profit' and a 'fair days pay for a fair days work'. It also has had a significant impact on single mothers who are now trying to provide adequate care, due to the wages gap between men and women. We are now faced with an increasing level of poverty for single parent families.

Dr Jim Stanford, Director of the Centre for Future Work, claims that, 'The decline in "Labour Share", when contrasted to the fact that workers are producing more with each hour of output, visible in the rising productivity, is evidence that they don't have the bargaining power to win higher wages that go along with that productivity'. The decline in Labour Share in Australia is seen by commentators as severe by international standards. When this occurs, according to Stanford, the traditional implicit contract between workers and employers is broken. Stanford also believes that a 'systematic' effort by policy makers is required to rebuild and modernise the institutions that influence wages and the distribution of outcome. I would firmly add that we need a sizeable shift in our current values before such a 'systematic' process can be put in place.

The Bureau of Statistics figures in 2019 on the distribution of income revealed that the share accruing to the top one fifth of income earners increased while the share going to all other households in all other income quintiles fell or remained unchanged. The wealthiest 20% of Australian households received nearly 41% of all income in 2013/14 while the poorest fifth took home just 7.5%. The gap between the rich and the poor is a growing drag on our collective well-being as a community.

On 21 February 2020, a *Report on Australians Living in Poverty* was released by the University of NSW and the Australian Council of Social Services. This report concluded that 3.24 million Australians or 13.6% of the population are living below the poverty line in Australia. These figures include 774,000 children under the age of fifteen years or 17.7% of the population, who are living below the poverty line. The reports leading researcher, Professor Bruce Bradbury, claims that the poverty rate in Australia is worse than in most wealthy countries, including Germany, New Zealand and Ireland.

They also conclude that this problem could be alleviated if the national government increased income support and assistance with housing and unemployment which would also include those who are underemployed.

As a result of the current income inequality, many families who are trying to cope with rising energy prices and cost of living are suffering, particularly because of the prolonged static wage growth by having to decide whether they pay their energy bills or go without food. In a 2017 study conducted by Foodbank Australia, the CEO Brianna Casey reported that more than one in five children in Australia lives in a food insecure household. Further, that one in three parents (32%) say that their children do not have enough to eat, at least once each month.

The main cause of household food insecurity (52%) is the rising cost of living which often forces parents to choose between paying their bills and feeding their families. Many parents (9 out of 10) in this study have had to make this choice, which occurs on a weekly basis for many of these families. In late 2018, the Liberal/National government in Australia actually cut significant funds from this organisation only to be publicly shamed into returning the grant within a matter of days.

Apart from the physical health implications of a diet imbalance, Food Security also reduces psychological stress in families; and it promotes positive, healthy, growth-promoting, social relationships because people who feel secure are more likely to reach out with love to others. In conclusion, these reports show that the gap between the rich and the poor is impacting on the collective wellbeing of our community. This is a 'distributive justice' issue that needs to be addressed because it can no longer be claimed, without question, that the creation of wealth for a few will inevitably benefit the many.

The inequality in the distribution of wealth has also led to the rising problem of 'homelessness'. First, in Australia, the Australian Bureau of Statistics revealed that on any given night, there are more than 105,000 people homeless. In Victoria alone, this figure is almost 23,000, comprising 13,000 males and 10,000 females. This includes 11,000 who are sleeping rough each night. Included in these figures are more than 3600 children under the age of 12 years. The ABS states that on any given night in Australia 1 in 200 people is homeless. Of course, these figures only reflect those who have been identified, and do not include the many people whose homeless situation remains hidden from the public view.

Wayne Merritt, who manages Frontyard Youth Services for the Melbourne City Mission, has summed up the core issue in his quote, 'We do not work with homeless people as such, but people who are experiencing homelessness'. Note the emphasis that Wayne makes when he says we are dealing with 'people first'. This is the sense of compassion that we need to encourage.

Another major social evil that appears to be on the rise in communities across the world is 'racial hatred'. When we witness the violent white rights demonstrations in America and Australia, we need to ask the question, have we gone back to the white supremacists attitude of the 60s, complete with the rise of the Klu Klux Klan and the Australian United Patriots Front?

Racism takes many forms and can happen anywhere. Racism includes prejudice, discrimination or hatred directed at someone because of the colour of their skin, ethnicity, national origin or religious beliefs. Most people associate racism with acts of physical violence or harassment; however, racism does not need to involve violent or intimidating behaviour, for example racial name-calling or jokes about race can equally be racist. Racism occurs when people are discriminated against and excluded because of their skin colour or ethnic background. Hence racism can be revealed through people's attitudes as well as their actions, it can also be reflected in the systems and institutions of the community. Racism occurs when people are prevented from being offered dignity, equality and respect simply because of their race. Racism can be subtle and it is not always blatant when people are being maligned. It is the responsibility of each individual to call out racist attitudes when they are presented. In 2020, resulting from the death of an African American by a police officer, we have seen a rise in the protest of this violence under the banner 'Black Lives Matter' which has awakened people to this evil right across the world.

People are not born with racist attitudes – these are learnt from people around us. There are some people including Australians who firmly believe that certain races are superior to others, and claim it is important that certain races should not mix with certain others. This belief in racial superiority can lead to racial hatred.

One of the most significant factors in the rise of racism is a fear based on ignorance. Fear of the unknown can cause anxiety, which leads to defensive reactions. Clearly, there are times when acts of racism are committed not through anger but through ignorance, unfortunately they are no less harmful. As the Gospel of Truth 10:12 (a sacred document found at Nag Hammadi) affirms, 'Ignorance dissolves when one gains knowledge of another'.

Research indicates that as many as 20% of Australia's population have experienced racial discrimination. Some Australians experience racial abuse more frequently than others, such as Aboriginal and Torres Strait Islanders and those from culturally diverse backgrounds such as Asians. These people also have to deal with the systemic forms of discrimination as well as the personal abuse. The history of racism in Australia has often been supported by government intervention such as the removal of children from indigenous families and the incarceration of indigenous people for minor offences. The separation of individuals from families and communities has caused emotional trauma for the families and communities as well as pain and suffering for the individuals. The many social and psychological problems that have resulted from such actions have led to damaging health issues, including mental illness and high rates of suicide.

Racism can occur anywhere and at anytime, be it at a shopping centre, sporting venue, workplace or on public transport. Often, the public media and especially radio 'shock jocks' are responsible for inciting racial violence. This is especially true when young African or indigenous

Australian youth commit violent crimes as we witnessed in Melbourne in 2018.

Unfortunately, this racial stereotyping occurs frequently and includes asylum seekers and refugees. Unfortunately, when this occurs, the community tars all people from these ethnic groups with the same brush.

A paper presented at Queensland University of Technology by Race Discrimination Commissioner Dr Helen Szoke reported that 27% of Aboriginal and Torres Strait Islanders over the age of 15 years experienced racial discrimination by the general public and three out of four experience racial discrimination when accessing primary health care. This research also revealed that people born overseas experienced higher incidents of racism than those born in Australia, and were twice as likely to experience racism in the workplace. This was especially true of people who had recently arrived in Australia. The report also discovered that racial discrimination decreases with the length of Australian residence. This report also revealed that Arabs, Muslims, Jews, Palestinians, Turkish and African Australians experience a higher risk of discrimination and prejudice which had previously been reserved for Asians.

Racism undermines social cohesion within the community. To ensure that social inclusion occurs, individuals need the opportunity to secure employment and access to health services and time to connect socially and spiritually with family and friends. Personal integrity depends on ready access to these opportunities. Racism also impacts adversely on the development of a multi-cultural Australia, which politicians of all persuasions continue to claim is an important value for every society. To be a truly democratic society, Australia must ensure that all people are considered free and experience equal rights. As is proclaimed in a song that for some people has become an unofficial national anthem. This song was written by Bruce Woodley who was a member of The Seekers, an Australian Pop quartet.

> We are one but we are many.
> And from all the lands on earth we come.
> We'll share a dream and sing with one voice.
> I am, you are, we are Australians.

Even though Australia is a signatory to the international convention on the elimination of racial discrimination, its lack of political recognition of the rights of indigenous Australians and asylum seekers has been appalling. The *Racial Discrimination Act* of 1975 which aims to promote inclusion and equality before the law is something that indigenous Australians and new arrivals to our shores have not experienced.

Australians must recognise that to fulfil our obligation under the 1975 Act we must first of all recognise and embrace that we share a common humanity with these people. It is the responsibility of every individual to respect with dignity the right of all people to be included in all opportunities for personal growth and fulfilment.

Most Australians have been made aware that many of our indigenous sporting greats are still receiving racial slurs. Eddie Betts, a player with the Australian Football League team Carlton, has made public his concern that opposition supporters have thrown him bananas during the game, insinuating that he is an 'ape'. A football follower was later summoned to front the Magistrates court because it was alleged she posted a racist comment on 'Facebook' by calling Eddie an 'ape'. A further comment on public media suggested that Betts should, 'Go back to the zoo where he and his family belong'.

Following these incidents, Betts posted on his Instagram that he would not let racism stand in his way when he wrote, 'I will keep going ... I have a job to do, inspiring our next generation to be the best they can be and making a change for our people...'

When the Aboriginal Australian Rules footballer and Australian of the Year, Adam Goodes began to challenge the racism of being called an 'ape' by a young football follower, he was criticised by sporting and social commentators such as Eddie McGuire and Andrew Bolt. This public attack led to Goodes being booed by football crowds following his Aboriginal war dance in the celebration of kicking a goal. The attack by these people was so ferocious that it caused depression for Goodes and, as a result, he chose to end his 372 game career, without the traditional farewell lap.

From 2017 to 2018, there was a 59% increase in anti-Semitic incidents which included 'harassment', through threats by mail and telephone and vandalism through the use of 'posters' and 'stickers' publicly displayed, especially in Jewish communities. Jews are consistently and verbally abused and harassed around synagogues particularly on Holy Days and Jewish festivals.

Basically, Australia remains a stable, vibrant and tolerant democracy, where Jews face no official discrimination and are free to practise their faith and traditions but, as we have discovered in Melbourne in 2019 and 2020, anti-Semitism still exists and a number still experience racial harassment and in some cases physical violence. It was reported recently that a group of young Jewish students whilst on their way home from school were verbally abused and physically threatened by a group of students of Anglo-Saxon origin travelling on public transport.

Anti-Semitism, like all racist attacks, must be 'called out' by political and community leaders, as well as by the wider public, as totally unacceptable. Until we all make a stand against anti-Semitism, these incidents will continue to threaten all who are subjected to this evil activity. The ideology of fear and the incitement to hatred is never acceptable in our nation or anywhere. It is our responsibility to name racism wherever we encounter it, be it at work, the dinner table, on public transport, on a Facebook page; and, further, to strongly declare that it is totally unacceptable to denigrate anyone simply because of their ethnic origin.

Unfortunately, many of our political leaders have used racist statements for purely political ends. A technique often referred to as 'dog whistling' has been used by a number of Australian politicians with the aim of inciting fear of those who are of a different ethnic origin. At times, playing the racist card for political purposes has bordered on xenophobia. Such a concern came to the fore in August 2018 when a senior government minister Peter Dutton, Minister for Home Affairs, raised fears of young African refugees from the Sudan who had been involved in violent robberies, carjacking and house invasions. This same minister claimed that people in Melbourne were too afraid to go out for dinner at night because of these occurrences.

As a result, because many of the crimes were violent, the Federal Government placed a hold on the refugee intake of young Sudanese men.

In response to these matters, while speaking to reporters in August 2018, the Victorian Premier Daniel Andrews stated, 'We know there are a large number of young people and the majority of these asylum seekers have lower levels of education than any other single group of refugees that have arrived in Australia'. (Victoria is where the largest number of young Sudanese have resettled.) Further, 'a majority of these young people had spent up to ten years in refugee camps under appalling conditions. Most have survived war torn brutal conflict situations. To top it off, they are attempting to learn how to settle into a culture vastly different from the one they have come from'.

From a purely pragmatic viewpoint, creating an atmosphere of fear for political purposes by claiming the streets of Melbourne are unsafe as a result of the actions of some Sudanese youths does not match with the factual crime statistics of the Victorian Police Force. The statistics of the Police Force revealed that the crime rate in August 2018 was down considerably and that there had been an increase in the number of police on the beat. These figures were revealed in the editorial section of the *Melbourne Age* on 23 December 2018. The editor also stated that figures of people dining out in Melbourne had not decreased and that the minister's comments were 'ill-informed and racially divisive'.

As a community, we must ensure that false fear-mongering statements by politicians for purely political reasons must never victimise the innocent or cower the community for embracing others who are ethnically different. We need to encourage all people in responsible positions to adopt the values of the Historical Jesus, because 'There are lies, damned lies and political statements' (With apologies to Benjamin Disraeli).

Another real concern is the support for people who propagate 'hate speech' such as the tour authorised for the British journalist Milo Yiannopoulos based on the statement that as Australians we support 'Free Speech'. Australia does not have a 'Bill of Rights' and so we have no official statement regarding a definition of 'Free Speech'.

Yiannopolous' extreme and at times irrational views are deliberately designed to incite neo-Nazis and misogynists to violence, through his tirades against women, indigenous people and Muslims.

Moira Rayner, barrister and writer, has stated that, 'The people of "Australasia" are at a crossroads. If we sow the seeds of hate, through dog whistling and hate speech, we will reap the consequences. It's time to build a caring society, otherwise we will tear ourselves apart'.

It is important to realise that 'words' matter; they have the power to hurt or to heal, divide or unite, to shed truth or disperse falsehood, especially when they come from prominent people in our community.

We need to consider the importance of encouraging a different set of values, such as those we find in the words and actions of the sage Jesus of Nazareth. It is the acknowledgment of these values that underpin supportive personal relationships, which need to be affirmed if we are to reduce the impact of the many social evils that exist in our society today. We will examine these values in greater detail later in the book.

In a recent article in November 2019, Deshna Charron Shine, Director of *ProgressiveChristianity.org* writes, 'These are crucial times for the planet we call home. The toxic and institutionalised systems of racism, tribalism, colonialism, cultural appropriation, sexism, and the general oppression of marginalised people have been thrust to the surface of our society... These are systems and beliefs Jesus faced and why he was crucified'.

How then do we resolve these social evils and do we need to change the way we live if we want to change the world? My conclusion is that yes, we do need to change the world but, you may ask, how can we, as individuals, make the world a better place when we do not have the power to do so? I would argue that the power to change our world lies within us as proclaimed by the historical Jesus.

Jesus demonstrated that the spiritual power of love within each of us could empower us to develop more compassionate, caring and loving relationships with all those with whom we engage. This is not an easy task as Jesus himself discovered primarily because there are many people in our community, particularly those who are in powerful roles, who will be threatened by the possibility of being challenged by those who are empowered by love. People will feel empowered if they are warmly regarded and loved;

and these feelings will generate a desire to ensure others are also empowered.

If we can encourage relationships of compassion in those we meet, then this will change our world regardless of the powerful political social and religious systems of our day which, unfortunately have allowed these evils to manifest themselves.

Chapter 7

Social Commentaries on the Current Circumstances

I HAVE INCLUDED THIS CHAPTER on social commentaries with the aim of addressing the often asked question, 'What if anything has changed in the Australian culture that contributes to the rise of these social evils?' To convey the message of social analysts and to explore this important question, I will conclude with chosen commentaries by three well-known and highly regarded social commentators, Mike Carlton, Richard Flanagan and Andrew Hamilton.

While the evidence from psychologists and social workers supports the belief that the influence of positive growth-promoting friendship can prevent many of the social evils we are currently facing in the twenty-first century, there are other factors in our society that need to be examined. My own research has shown that many social analysts are conveying, in a far more logical and practical way, the 'ethical' message of the historical Jesus than are a number of orthodox Christian theologians.

These researchers have also discovered in their surveys that majority of Australians are egalitarian in their approach to the needs of others rather than totalitarian. In his writings, Hugh Mackay emphasises this fact.

If we aim to decrease the social evils that pervade our life, then we need also to explore whether Australia's historical development and the structure of our society and its institutions fully support the evidence of the value of compassionate and caring relationships.

In my own discussions with people who are involved in faith communities, they were concerned that the egalitarian message of Jesus is rejected not only by politicians but also by leaders in business and social activities. They were also critical of the lack of regard and compassion for children in orthodox Christian institutions.

The examples they gave were based on the findings from the Royal Commission into Institutional Child Sexual Abuse, released on 15 December 2017. A general concern from my Catholic friends was that their church was more concerned about maintaining its empire than protecting and caring for the children in its care.

If we examine the causes behind such issues as 'violence against women' and the failure to recognise that women should be recognised as having equal rights to men; or the social issue of racism and in particular its impact on our own indigenous Australians and Australia's response to asylum seekers, we may discover, by examining the detailed research from our own social analysts and researchers, that we will need to reinterpret an understanding of our history and become more compassionate to those who have suffered under our political and social systems.

In relation to the abuse of women one only has to remember how Julia Gillard, Australia's first female Prime Minister, was treated by her political rivals who referred to her as a 'witch', when they supported signs at a rally stating 'Ditch The Witch'. Then there was the right wing political commentator Alan Jones from radio station 2GB suggesting that she should be 'put in a chaff bag and thrown into the sea.' All of these comments would have been encouragement to aggressive males who believed they had a right to physically abuse women.

The evidence I received from orthodox Christians – especially from members of the Catholic Church – was a major concern regarding the lack of equal rights for women, whether this was in the participation of worship services or in administrative decision-making. A number of Catholic females who provided me with information even suggested that, because the church did not regard women as equal to men, it encouraged men to believe they were more powerful and therefore had the right to abuse their female partners.

Another issue of major concern was Australia's response to the needs of people seeking asylum. Since the 1980s, the Australian government has failed to show the values compassion and empathy for those people fleeing violent circumstance and seeking asylum and safety in Australia.

This lack of support for people seeking asylum flies in the face of the government's commitment to the conditions of being a member of the United Nations after having signed the Declaration of Human Rights, which declares in article 14:

> (1) Everyone has the right to seek and to enjoy in other countries asylum from persecution.
>
> (2) This right may not be invoked in the case of prosecutions genuinely arising from non-political crimes or from acts contrary to the purposes and principles of the United Nations.

This approach by the Australian Government has caused some critics to now regard our government as 'morally incoherent'.

Julian Burnside is a well-known and highly regarded lawyer and advocate for the rights of asylum seekers. In his book *Watching Brief Reflecting on Human Rights, Law, and Justice*, he articulates a sensitive and legal defence of the rights of asylum-seekers and refugees but, more importantly, he stresses the importance of totally protecting human rights and maintaining the rule of law.

The rights of Indigenous Australians and in particular their ownership of the land is also a contentious issue, which for many indigenous Australians has caused them to question their allegiance to Australian citizenship. A number of Indigenous leaders refuse to recognise Australia Day because it is a celebration of the landing in Australia of the Englishman Captain James Cook. Some of these leaders refer to this day celebrated on 26 January as 'Invasion Day' because they believe that the land was stolen from them.

Those who are old enough will remember that in the 1970's just after the Whitlam government was elected in 1972, there was an intense debate regarding the land rights of indigenous Australians.

Gough Whitlam's 1972 election campaign speech was clear on the need to accord Aboriginal and Torres Strait Islander peoples the rights, justice and opportunities that had been denied to them for so long.

He articulated a commitment which was we need to: 'legislate to give Aborigines land rights – not just because their case is beyond argument, but because all of us as Australians are diminished while the Aborigines are denied their rightful place in this nation'.

He argued that Australians 'ought to be angry – with an unrelenting anger – that our Aborigines have the world's highest infant mortality rate.' Indigenous Affairs was therefore the policy area in which the Whitlam Government effected some of its most transformational change. Under the Whitlam Government, a policy of 'self determination' was adopted, whereby the Commonwealth would support decision-making by Aboriginal and Torres Strait Islander peoples themselves, and relinquish the paternalistic control that previous governments had wielded over the lives of Australia's First Nations Peoples.

The Whitlam Government sought to empower Aboriginal and Torres Strait Islander peoples to claim back the land to which they were entitled, to allow them more input into policy-making, and to abolish discriminatory practices that limited their freedoms and opportunities. The Fraser

Government continued many of these reforms initiated by the Whitlam Government.

There was a reaction to the Whitlam Government's decision to give land rights to indigenous Australians from some right wing politicians, who used a scare campaign, which claimed that the indigenous Australians would take over the houses of white Australians. Fortunately, the liberal party under Malcolm Fraser who was a strong supporter of the Whitlam Government's legislation ensured the legislation regarding indigenous land rights would continue regardless of the scare campaign, which was supported by some of his party members.

Hence the evidence is clear that unless political and community leaders adopt the values of compassion as expressed by Jesus of Nazareth it will make the solving of the social evils that were raised earlier more difficult. Hence as companions of Jesus and believers in the empowering influence of friendship, there will be times when we need to confront our leaders, be they politicians, community or religious leaders. It will be our responsibility to encourage our leaders to ensure that the well being of all people is their highest priority.

Let us now examine the writings of three other social analysts as we continue to explore the question, 'What if anything has changed in the Australian culture that contributes to the rise of these social evils?' I have also included the study conducted by Rebecca Huntley because the results of this study strongly support the commentaries of the social researchers and analysts.

Mike Carlton is a journalist, broadcaster and author of naval history. I am referring primarily to Carlton's commentary in his article, 'The Land of the Fair Gone', which was published in the Saturday Paper, 31 March 2018. At the beginning of his article, he uses the example of players in the Australian cricket team illegally tampering with the cricket ball to gain an advantage. It is significant that Carlton would use this example, primarily because cricket in Australia is very much a part of the fabric of who we are. Further, the game of cricket from an international perspective, is regarded to have a set of unwritten principles about fair play.

In Australia, we are very familiar with the term 'It's just not cricket', which means someone has not acted in accordance with the principles of the game. This is perhaps why the international response was to condemn not only the actions of the three cricketers involved, but the whole Australian cricket administrative structure for creating an atmosphere that 'winning at all costs' was more important than adhering to the principles of the game. The concern for many Australians was that the illusion that our sporting heroes were morally spotless had now been shattered.

Carlton claims that the cheating by members of the Australian cricket team is merely a symptom of a much wider national sickness. He suggests that there is now a culture of greed, selfishness, envy and cruelty that is growing at the heart of the nation. He raises the question, 'Whatever happened to our firmly held belief that in Australia the concept of a 'fair go' was inherent in our culture?' The evils of greed, selfishness, envy and cruelty have become supreme.

Selfishness brings with it the denial of the rights of others. Carlton suggests that these evils are widespread and that the cheating at cricket is but one example. The rejection of the culture of a 'fair go' is also occurring in our political system.

In support of this claim, Carlton refers to recent examples of political situations that confirm John Kenneth Galbraith's dictum: 'The modern conservative is engaged in one of man's oldest exercises in moral philosophy: that is, the search for a superior moral justification for their own selfishness'. Carlton is also concerned that the financial theory of 'Trickle Down' promulgated by the federal government is simply not working.

As pointed out in the last chapter, wages growth is at its lowest since World War II. Hence the Prime Minister's corporate tax cuts, according to the Business Council of Australia, have not led to wages growth as predicted. As a result, many families are now dipping into life savings in order to feed their families and pay their bills. The Business Council reported that 80% of companies used their profits by lining the pockets of the shareholders or investing profit back into the company rather than increasing wages. I would add that some international companies in Australia are sending their profits offshore and in some situations this has meant avoiding paying tax on profits.

Carlton also raises his concern that a number of politicians and senior public servants have acted immorally. The examples he cites are from both sides of parliament and in both State and Federal governments – to the disgust of voters, because they 'loathe the arrogance and duplicity of their rulers'. Mike Carlton claims that as a result of these actions, decency and fairness in our culture are now dead. To justify this claim, he raises the example of Australia's Home Affairs Minister Peter Dutton and his treatment of refugees and Sudanese youth, as referred to earlier. Carlton says that Dutton's actions are in defiance not only of human decency but also of international law and common humanity.

The Home Affairs Minister is also criticised for his decisions to deny suicidal refugee children in detention centres the support they required in Australia while at the same time personally approving visas for visiting European au pairs. It took the actions of a judge to rescue a young Iranian boy from detention in Nauru.

Carlton expresses a deep concern about Australia's attitude to young indigenous Australians, especially those who have been incarcerated for minor offences. He states that more than half the juveniles in Australian jails are indigenous and are products of a third-world squalor. There have been times when they have been denied legal aid. Such is the trauma of their incarceration and isolation from community that a significant number have taken their own lives. Carlton compares Australia's lack of financial support to our indigenous community with the billions of dollars that are being given to wealthy private schools.

In this article, he also challenges the large companies who avoid paying taxes by shifting profits offshore. These include the financial organisations mentioned in the last chapter who refuse to pay their workers minimum wages and at the same time refuse to accept responsibility for paying the legally entitled superannuation. On top of this the company executives in a number of these organisations are paid millions of dollars.

We are witnessing more and more young Australians snared in the so-called gig economy of low paid casual labour that doesn't include holiday or sick pay, superannuation or, most importantly, job security. In support of his concern about economic inequality, Carlton raises the issue of the corruptness of the big banks and large financial institutions, detailed by the Royal Commission Into Misconduct in the Banking, Superannuation and Financial Services Industry. This report was finalised in February 2019 and it found that a number of these companies were involved in money laundering for criminal gangs and in the charging of services that were never supplied. Carlton's major concern on these matters is that there has not been an appropriate monitoring system with the legislative powers to hold these institutions to account.

As Carlton points out, it is not just politicians and business executives who are causing real concern for the community, but also institutions that in the past have been relied on for fairness and moral coherency, such as the Christian churches. The Royal Commission into child sexual abuse by church leaders has shown that not only did abuse occur at an alarming rate, but church leaders attempted to cover this abuse by making small compensation payments, on the condition that the victims did not go to the civil authorities or the general public.

Other reports have revealed that child abuse has also been occurring in indigenous communities and as an outcome of domestic violence generally.

Mike Carlton's article is an attempt to discover a trigger for Australia's demise from a proudly egalitarian society that took pride in the value of a 'fair go' to the disastrous situation we find ourselves in today. He is 'inclined' to date the beginning of this demise to the prime ministership of John Howard, primarily because, Carlton believes, it was Howard who supported the elevation of 'selfishness' and 'xenophobia' as national virtues, which under his leadership were used for political purposes.

I would add that these so-called virtues have also provided fertile ground for the rise of white supremacy and hate speech. Even though Carlton is a journalist, he does not resile from including criticism of the mainstream media, and in particular 'Murdoch's news group'. There, he claims, 'vendetta' journalism has become something of an art form. Carlton lists the prominent women in Australia who have been targets of this relentless bullying. His list includes former Prime Minister Julia Gillard, young Muslim activist and engineer Yasmin Abdel-Magied, former Human Rights Commissioner Gillian Triggs and indigenous academic Larissa Behrendt. The ABC's economic journalist Emma Alberici was attacked by the Murdoch Press until the ABC had her dismissed from her position. The Murdoch Press had targeted all of these women.

According to Carlton, a primary form of attack by John Howard was to label any form of compassion as 'political correctness' or 'virtue signalling' and this verbal attack was used against any idea that he or his acolytes didn't agree with.

So where to from here? Carlton suggests that the only way forward out of this 'mess' is for genuine leadership to return Australia to being that country where there is at least a halfway decent chance of getting and giving the 'fabled fair go'. Carlton does not consider any of our current political leaders capable of leading our country forward, which will require a commitment to a morally coherent and compassionate approach, particularly for those who are disadvantaged.

Another well-regarded social analyst is Richard Flanagan. In his address to the National Press Club, he examined a divided Australia, which has deserted a spirit of true social democracy. Flanagan proposed that our country could only be truly democratic when it is willing to face up to the problems of its history. The title of his address was, 'Our Politics is a Dreadful Black Comedy'.

He begins his analysis with a joke about a man doubled up in front of Parliament House, violently throwing up. A stranger walking past places his arm around the vomiting man and says, 'I know how you feel'. This is a classical illustration about a failing regime that has lost the essential moral legitimacy that is needed to govern the country.

Flanagan compares the political situation in Australia to that of Yugoslavia in the 1980s following the death of Marshall Tito, when a financial crisis became a political crisis. When the politicians were unable to find solutions, they pitched neighbour against neighbour. The situation quickly descended into nationalistic and ethnic hatreds, and concluded with what became a genocidal madness. Richard witnessed this terrible situation as a young man and realised that the veneer of civilised societies is very thin. It is also 'fragile' and, once broken, releases 'monsters'.

Flanagan explains that Czechoslovakia under Vaclav Havel took a different approach after their revolution in 1989. Havel warned the West not to gloat about old Soviet states, as it could find itself in a similar 'existential crisis'. In Europe, we are now witnessing the rise of strong leaders, like Putin in Russia and Erdogan in Turkey, who, Flanagan suggests, are not saviours of democracy. Rather, around the world we see the growth of authoritarianism, which is always anti-democratic in practice, fascist in sympathy, rationalist in sentiment, and criminal in disposition. Its poisonous rhetoric is aimed at refugees, Muslims and increasingly towards the Jews. It is hostile towards truth and those who confront them with it, particularly journalists, which in some cases has led to murder.

In Australia, we may feel immune to these dangerous cultural/political conditions. We may be more concerned with politicians lining their own pockets and voting not for the good of the country but for their own personal needs. Nonetheless, this is far from a dictatorship. Even the rise of Hansonism in the 1990s has never threatened our democracy.

However, as Flanagan points out, we do have concerns about where we are heading as a nation, primarily due to the lack of social democratic political leaders. Positive leadership is lacking as our society grows more unequal by the day, more disenfranchised, angrier and fearful, as many are living without a sense of hope. The issues raised earlier – poverty, homelessness, abuse of women and children, and the growing gap between rich and poor – means that many people are living in fear for themselves and their children.

Instead of a rational public debate about these issues, the politicians offer up 'scapegoats' in the form of migrants and refugees who are labelled as 'illegal boat people', 'queue jumpers' and 'violent Muslims'. Both major political parties have used xenophobic fear. Where are our new visions, new ideas of how to be a compassionate caring community? What can we do to transform our nation and our people? The fundamental challenge posed by Flanagan is not about tax giveaways, negative gearing or public infrastructure. It is to realise that if we don't create for ourselves a liberating vision that is grounded in the full truth of who we are as a people, we will find ourselves in a moment of crisis, suddenly trapped in a new authoritarianism and finding comfort in the old lies of our history.

According to Flanagan, much of Australia's national pride has been built on lies. He cites the situation in Australia of honouring, almost religiously, Anzac Day as a classic because the truth we need to recognise is that the 62,000 young men who died in World War I far from their own land did so in the service of a distant Empire fighting another Empire. Yet the Federal government allocated $100 million on a war museum in France named after Sir John Monash.

Flanagan suggests also that if we truly want to honour patriots for giving their lives for their land, we should spend that $100 million on a museum for the estimated 65,000 indigenous Australians who tragically lost their lives defending their country in the 'frontier wars' of the 1880s. We need to face the truth of who we are, which means we must face the truth of our past. We need to accept that the prosperity of modern Australia has been built on the exploitation and destruction of Australia's first people. We need to tell their story and honour their contribution for the nurture of this land. We need to value their 'dreamings', sayings, languages, and their methods to renew the cosmos.

One of our first duties is to encourage the development of a national indigenous advisory body to the Australian government and to ensure that their contribution to our land is recognised by the Australian Constitution. We cannot progress as a nation until these matters are resolved, and we cannot hope to be a republic if our recognition of our indigenous people doesn't provide the core of our constitution. At the moment the date of our Australia Day honours the landing of the British Captain James Cook. As long as this continues, it will divide Australia.

The Uluru Statement offers us a chance to complete our democracy to make it stronger, more inclusive and more robust. We need a large and open vision sustained in truth, not myths that encourage dangerous illusions. For twenty years, Australia has lived with the definition that we are selfish, xenophobic, homophobic and incapable of grasping larger visions. It was the marriage equality debate that proved this is no longer so. Since that vote, it is clear that Australians are not the mean, pinched people we had been persuaded we were.

We are not small-minded bigots, we are people who care and think and, most importantly, people who feel for the needs of others.

Flanagan concludes that we can now offer the invitation to dream, because our country belongs to 'dreamers'. The message of his social analysis is abundantly clear: if Australia is to fulfil its potential as a morally coherent nation, it must first of all face the reality of its long held myths.

First, we will never be truly one nation if we cannot include and show respect for the rights of our nation's first people. We are not the egalitarian, compassionate country we claim to be if we cannot accept the rights of indigenous Australians. Our historical response to the land rights, education, legal justice, health and welfare needs of our first people have been shameful and have even bordered on genocide. The prolonged resistance of our political leaders to publicly apologise for the harm the Australian authorities inflicted on families by the removal of their children, is another example of our lack of compassion.

There has also been a continued refusal by politicians to accept the Uluru Statement, which is called 'A Statement from the Heart'. This seeks to obtain constitutional reform with the aim of empowering indigenous Australians, so that their rightful place in their own country is politically and publicly recognised. (See Appendix A for the full statement.)

Further, we can no longer live with the belief that our young men who were sacrificed on the battlefields of Anzac Cove and France did so defending their country, when they were defending the British Empire. Unfortunately, many of their injuries and fatalities were the result of poor leadership. This in no way suggests that we should not mourn their sacrifice and support their families, but that we need to place this response in perspective.

I can still remember, as a primary school child, singing the Bene Gibson Smyth song:

> We will remember them today,
> Who from their homeland sailed away.
> So blithely and so willingly
> To give their lives for you and me.
> Father, guard their sleeping.

My father had fought in France in World War I but my logic told me that these young men were not in reality defending Australia, so were they giving their lives for me?

The third social analyst I wish to examine is Andrew Hamilton, a commentator with *Eureka Street*, an on-line news publication sponsored by the Catholic Jesuit community. In volume 28 number 13, he raises the question, 'Whatever happened to 'kindness to strangers'?'

This article refers to the Australian Government's response to people seeking protection and asylum as part of the international punitive policy handed out to such people in need. The Australian government's treatment of refugees and asylum seekers in their offshore detention centres on Manus Island and Nauru coincides with Italy's refusal to receive refugees and the separation of children from their parents of Latin American refugees that occurred in the USA.

These events are sometimes attributed to a failure in political leadership but, as Hamilton suggests, they reflect a deeper cultural change in Western society's attitude to strangers. This smacks of an almost international xenophobia.

These manifestations are seen not only in migrant and refugee policy statements, but also in Australia's penal policy and international relations. As an example, the Australian Government reduced significantly its contribution to overseas aid in five successive budgets.

So why have these changes in cultural attitude taken place? Hamilton compares our attitude to strangers with the more generous attitude that prevailed after the Second World War. Then, European leaders sought to work cooperatively in sharing the burden of care for the refugees displaced as a result of seven years of conflict.

These leaders recognised the disastrous consequences of xenophobic nationalism, often disguised today as 'patriotism'. They also recognised the need for a just and compassionate international order that was rule-based and attended to the needs of those who had been disadvantaged.

This vision for a more compassionate world found expression in institutions like the United Nations, international trade organisations and the European Union. It is also found in the expanded role of governments in accepting responsibility to shape a more compassionate society. In particular, this was expressed through the United Nations Refugee Convention. International cooperation was essential in the response to the millions of people displaced as a result of the wars in Europe.

It is interesting to note that many European leaders were motivated to respond to this crisis by their Christian understanding of the message of Jesus in accepting responsibility for the poor and the stranger.

Hamilton points to the post-war vision of a better world enshrined in the value of 'hospitality to strangers', which saw in them possibilities rather than threats. This clearly was a vision of a world that included strangers, rather than excluding them. It allowed for relationships to develop, which in turn reduced the feeling of isolation. Our nine-year-old grandson Harrison gave a class presentation on the subject of 'A Multicultural Australia' which was videotaped. During the presentation, he referred to his grandmother's work supporting and teaching English to refugee families. He concluded that, 'the most important thing his grandmother did was to make these people feel that they belonged'.

The vision for a more humane world also included providing penal policies that emphasised rehabilitation over punishment, as well as refugee policies that emphasised inclusion within society, rather than assimilation. In most cases, these new values had success but, as Hamilton points out, this vision has now faded. International organisations such as the United Nations and its associate bodies concerned with human rights and refugees are now judged purely by whether they support the national interests of particular nations.

Australia's federal government has – by merging the departments of Defence and Immigration to establish their program 'Operation Sovereign Borders' – ensured that the media cannot question any activity regarding refugees attempting to come to Australia by boat because it is now a part of our defence forces. This has given rise to a selfish nationalism.

The institutional changes that have been made in Australia and worldwide reflect a broader suspicion and in some cases a fear of strangers. Some politicians claim that refugees who arrive must be considered as rivals with Australians for jobs and health services. Further, these arrivals are to be considered as 'threats' rather than offering 'possibilities'. In the main, the government's reaction has been control through exclusion, rather than to see the arrivals of refugees as opportunities for learning and growth and development.

Suspicion breeds fear and fear breed's hostility. This leads to the rise of white supremacists and preaching racial hatred, followed by acts of violence towards refugees and asylum seekers. A government reinforces these fears when it labels refugees, even those fleeing hostility, as a threat that can only be controlled by the country's armed forces.

The legislative and policy hardening in the Australian attitude to strangers seeking asylum will not quickly be reversed. Our only hope is that, at some point, people will begin to recognise that as Australians we have both a moral and ethical responsibility to the strangers who come to our shores seeking protection for themselves and their families.

Most importantly of all, Australians must realise that our current attitudes to the stranger in our midst will endanger and impoverish our community. For a change to happen, we will require morally coherent and ethically aware political and social leaders, who know that a generous and compassionate society is founded on just, compassionate and hospitable personal relationships.

In his 2018 book *Australia Reimagined: Towards a more compassionate, less anxious society*, esteemed social researcher Hugh Mackay argues intelligently that the underlying cause of the social problems we face today, and which create incredible anxiety, are a result of the lack of compassion, empathy and inclusivity in our personal relationships. His book also challenges Australians to accept responsibility to create a more healthy community by encouraging people to be more compassionate, generous, cohesive, and inclusive at the local neighbourhood level.

When we say it is our responsibility to offer hospitality to the alien and stranger, what exactly do we mean? And where does this impetus come from? First, as Australians, our government has committed us to the United Nations Universal Declaration of Human Rights, which defines a refugee as:

> Any person who owing to a well-founded fear of being persecuted for reasons of race, religion, nationality, membership of a particular social group or political opinion, is outside the country of his/her nationality and is unable, or owing to such fear, is unwilling to avail himself/herself of the protection of that country.

Thus, by simply being an Australian, we have a responsibility to refugees, regardless of our religious beliefs, because our country is a signatory to the 'Convention relating to the status of Refugees'. If you like, it is our civil responsibility.

When we say that it is our responsibility to offer 'hospitality', what does this mean? A simple definition of hospitality is: 'The quality or disposition of receiving and treating guests and strangers in a warm and friendly way'.

However, as we are people from a Judeo-Christian heritage, does this mean that more is being asked of us? Let us briefly turn to both the Old and New Testaments for assistance in understanding our responsibilities.

The Jewish instructions respecting strangers/aliens pervade all the writings of the Hebrew Bible from its community history through to the Torah and the prophets.

For example, in Leviticus 19:34 we read:

> The stranger/alien who resides with you shall be to you as the native among you and you shall love him (them) as yourself; for you were aliens in the land of Egypt; I am the Lord your God.

And in Deuteronomy 14:29 we read:

> The Levites, because they have no allotment or inheritance with you, as well as the resident aliens, the orphans and the widows in your towns, may come and eat their fill so that the Lord your God may bless you in all the work that you undertake.

In Job 31:32:

> The Stranger/Alien has not lodged in the street.
> I have opened my doors to the traveller.

The New Testament adds an even greater demand on us regarding the stranger/alien or person in need. The most appropriate translation of the English word 'hospitality' is from the Greek word philoxenia which means a 'love' of the guest or stranger. The emphasis is not just on what we do, but on how we personally regard the one in need. Our hospitality should be a way of life and an embrace of the other, rather than a simple response to someone in need.

Our response to people in need is perhaps best brought to our attention by the words of Jesus, as recorded in Matthew 25:31ff:

> For I was hungry and you gave me food, I was thirsty and you gave me something to drink, I was a stranger and you welcomed me, I was naked and you gave me clothing, I was sick and you took care of me, I was in prison and you visited me... And when his disciples asked him, 'When was this?', he responded by saying: 'Truly I tell you as you did it to the least of these who are members of my family, you did it to me'.

The charge then is this: we must treat all we meet as if they are a loved one and by responding with love, we are responding to the Spirit of Jesus.

Is it possible that we need the stranger more than they need us? As Henri Nouwen suggests in his book *Reaching*

Out, 'hospitality is about offering a safe space where the stranger can enter and become a friend'. Hospitality is not designed to change people, but to offer a space where a relationship can take place. So the challenge to us as people of faith is clear: genuine hospitality is a deeply personal commitment to love the stranger. It is not some act we perform, but something that defines the people we are by the way we share our lives. Hospitality, then, is a way of living life and living it more abundantly, by sharing not only what we have but also, who we are.

With the global shift to the conservative right, where do the majority of Australians stand politically? Would the majority of Australians support a government that is committed to the values of social democracy and the values of Jesus of Nazareth?

Rebecca Huntley, in the *Quarterly Essay* titled 'Australia Fair: Listening to the Nation' (QE73, March 2019), analyses the results of her broad-ranging social research into the political values of the majority of Australians.

She begins with the claim that the role of governments is to 'update policy and law to reflect the views and desires of the democratic majority', and the main aim of 'social democracy' is to 'reconcile capitalism, democracy and social cohesion'. Hence the role of a socially democratic government is not just to do what is merely profitable but also, to do what is right for the community.

Huntley's research suggests that the social democratic policy that Australians desire requires not only a reform of taxation to make it more equitable, but also higher taxes across the board. Even in the vexed question of asylum seekers, Australians are seeking a less defensive and more open approach. Hence Australians in the future must be ready for reform and even more ready for a revival of a comprehensive social democracy.

However, as Huntley points out, any incoming government must be bold in its approach and unapologetic in its advocacy for the public sector. It must also be courageous in its approach to the environment and the issue of climate change if it is to achieve the social democratic government that many Australians are seeking.

Huntley's broad-ranging research shows that politicians are not 'poll driven' as is often claimed. If they were, previous Australian governments would have been listening to the desires of the populace and would have:

- Increased funding to the ABC.
- Made childcare more affordable.
- Made marriage equality a law by introducing it through parliament without the damaging and hurtful postal survey.
- Accepted the Uluru Statement from the Heart.
- Legalised euthanasia.
- Made more funding available for N.D.I.S. and Medicare.
- Endorsed the Gonski reforms.
- Ensured that Australia installed a world class NBN.

All of these issues attracted 60% of public support and, more importantly, there is basic agreement along party lines. The other fallacy about the attitude of the Australian nation is the belief that people have lost trust in politics, government and democracy. Trust in institutions is not at an all-time low. In reality, the evidence from social research is that Australians have never really trusted politicians. The *Essential Report* in 2018 reported that the most trusted institutions were Federal and State police (70% & 60%), the High Court (61%), the ABC (54%) and the Reserve Bank (50

We can gather from this data that Australians still have faith in institutions, particularly those that uphold the rule of law. It is the political parties that are at the lowest end of the trust list, scoring 15%.

In 2018, 27% of Australians (according to an Australian National University report) had 'no confidence at all in political parties and this number is declining'. The Australian Evaluation Society report showed that the proportion of Australians who agree that, 'People in government (politicians and public servants) can be trusted' has declined from 51% in 1969 to 26% in 2016.

Huntley's research affirms her belief that while a majority of Australians are disdainful of party politics, they are still vitally interested in political issues. Most of her focus group participants were interested in the big issues that face the Australian public. The supportive evidence for this conclusion can be found in the fact that 'informality' i.e., deliberate or accidental error in recording one's vote has decreased in recent years.

Enrolment to vote in the election in 2019 was higher than 97% of the eligible voting population. Since 1924, when voting was declared compulsory, the figure has been around 90% or more. This shows that voting is something that is widely embraced by the majority of Australians regardless of which generation they belong to.

While there is strong support for compulsory voting, focus groups have shown that most Australians would vote even if it weren't compulsory. Some political commentators claim that compulsory voting is the most consistent and distinctive character of the Australian system. It is also considered as the glue that keeps the democratic majority together.

Research quoted by Huntley from the Australian Voting System reveals that Australians are committed to the concept of democracy. It found that nine out of ten Australians believe that having a democracy that is 'very good' or 'fairly good' is the way forward. This figure has increased since 1995.

However, both major political parties from 2010 have replaced their leaders. These activities have led to 86% Australian population becoming less satisfied with democracy. This indicates that while Australians support the concept of democracy, they are not happy with how it is working in practice. By 2019, satisfaction with the democratic system had fallen significantly to 41

Trust in politicians is low and trust in other institutions is declining, but a majority of Australians still support the process that elects them to run our country. Huntley, reflecting on the results of her research, has resolved that good government is one that makes it hard to buy a gun and easier to get health care. Perhaps this is why social democracy still remains attractive to the Australian public.

Broadly speaking, this research supports the principle that social democratic policies are valued because they seek to ameliorate rather than dismantle capitalism, in the interest of equality and social justice. Further, social democracy relies on an elected government to protect all people, especially the working and middle classes.

Social democrats worldwide aim to reduce inequality caused by market forces. They do this by ensuring a minimum or living wage, compulsory arbitration, unemployment insurance, publicly funded education, health care, welfare support, public transport and public broadcasting. A socially democratic society must also provide services such as public pensions and develop systems providing support for people who, through no fault of their own, are unable to become competitive. For social democrats, life is far more important than being financially competitive. It is about friendships, love, passion, and family-life. Or, in the words of feminist Eva Cox, 'We live in a society not an economy'.

In Australia, 'social democracy' has not been fully realised and the vision of a fair and compassionate society has been compromised by our leaders' commitment to capitalism. Huntley suggests a number of reasons for this failure.

First, the changes implemented during the Hawke/Keating Government failed to persist because they did not build public confidence in the state as effective, efficient and profitable, while at the same time delivering the essential services to the whole population. As a result of the lack of community approval, social democratic reform was weakened.

Secondly, government reforms have not reduced economic inequality. In fact, as discussed in chapter 2, it is possible that in the last six years economic inequality has escalated.

This is supported by the Australian Council of Social Service report referred to by Huntley. It showed that economic inequality in Australia is above the OECD average. According to Huntley's research, this is a direct result of low wage growth, unaffordable housing, the gender pay gap, inadequate investment in health and education, inequalities in the tax systems, and insufficient welfare payments.

The third issue – which has damaged the potential for a socially democratic Australia – is the lack of trust in politicians. Many of our politicians are more concerned with their allegiance to their political party factions than they are to the needs of ordinary Australians, and of the nation as a whole.

A further concern, also raised in chapter 6, is the failure to take up a united fight against racism and hate speech. This has divided our sense of being a united nation. A similar argument can be put for the moral issue of global warming and climate change. Such is the divisiveness of this issue that it has led to the demise of at least three Prime Ministers.

If we are to rescue social democracy, we need to go back to the basic concern for the welfare of individuals, which must be a primary concern over and above economic outcomes. This is an ethical dilemma, which must be faced if we are to develop as a nation for all Australians and not just the wealthy minority.

According to Huntley's social research, Australians are far more concerned with the quality of life for all.

Personally, I often hear people say, 'I do not want or need tax cuts because I take my responsibility for the welfare of others seriously. My taxes provide the government with the resources necessary to make this a fair society.' The only concern I hear people voice regarding the paying of taxes is that they must be used efficiently and effectively and not abused by politicians.

As Huntley reports, when people were asked in 1969 whether they preferred less tax or more services, 65% said they favoured 'less tax'. In a recent *Essential Report*, 61% of respondents supported the same level of increased tax for more spending on services.

It is apparent from this research that a majority of Australians do not believe that the economic system of 'trickle down' is working. They supported (81%) revenue raising by closing the tax loopholes being exploited by large companies. They also said (70%) that revenue raising could be achieved by a higher income tax rate.

Overall, most people interviewed indicated that there are fundamental inequalities in the tax system and that these usually favour people on higher incomes.

If we believe in a social democratic political system, then budgets are moral documents. They signal what and whom we prioritise and seek to protect or uplift. As friends of Jesus of Nazareth, we can disagree on many issues but it should be hard to argue against the belief that there is an overriding call in the Bible to demonstrate a particular concern for the poor and prioritise the welfare of the vulnerable. This is the moral test by which we must evaluate every state budget, perhaps even more importantly the federal budget.

Chapter 8
The Role of Faith Communities

THE REALM OF GOD as defined by Jesus of Nazareth is a realm of radical inclusion, a society of radical equality. All people are welcome in the kingdom announced by Jesus, including those marginalised by society or whom Stephen Patterson refers to as the 'expendables'. These are the lepers, the sick, disabled, prostitutes and tax collectors. We read in Mark 2:16 that Jesus shares meals with tax collectors and sinners and challenges the purity code by declaring in Matthew 15:10-11: 'Listen and understand: it is not what goes into the mouth that defiles a person, but it is what comes out of the mouth that defiles'.

We all embark on tasks then wish that we hadn't, because it becomes all too hard. You try to walk away from the whole thing, but you find that it continues to nag at you until you go back and take up the cudgels again. When I first began to explore the historical Jesus in the late 1990s and tried to define what I believed the God Spirit was, it all seemed so exciting and straightforward. However, I quickly discovered that this wasn't the case. Whilst I was able to question the traditional interpretation given of Jesus' birth, the miracles and some of the sayings that were attributed to him, the logical consequence of what I did believe when these concerns were removed told much more about what I didn't believe. Would it have been better if I had continued to hold the faith of my teenage years and not be too critical about matters of reason and intellect?

The questioning began simply: I argued that if the God I believed in was not someone whose wrath brought tsunamis as a punishment for a wicked world, and this phenomenon could be explained by the science of massive earth movements under the sea, then could I call upon God to make other changes in our world? Could I ask God to heal my friend who has a massive brain tumour or heal a child involved in a car accident? It was so much easier as a teenager to talk about God as a personal being, a loving parent, rather than as 'essence' or a 'sea of love' or as Tillich says the 'ground of our being'. It was easier to talk about 'prayers of intercession' and handing over the responsibility of doing something to God than to meditate on how I could respond to the plight of my friends, the poor or disadvantaged and actually do something about it.

Could I continue to be blissfully ignorant and disregard these nagging doubts and their accompanying quests for openness and truth, or – having once been challenged – would this change my way of functioning forever? To face the reality that I do not know what God looks like and that the person of Jesus is a much more complex and confronting figure than we were taught at Sunday school was a daunting prospect.

I remember being in a study group with a group of people who had just studied Albert Nolan's book Jesus before Christianity and I posed the question, 'Could we change Jesus' mind on a particular issue?', 'Would he accept advice from us?' All of the group participants were considerably younger and all stated that Jesus' thinking was far above ours and that he would not have accepted our advice because he had the ability to foresee the outcomes we were postulating. If this is the case then is it possible that Jesus was just game playing with his disciples when he asked them questions and he already knew the answers? It would mean that when he invited us into discussions and debate, he wasn't interested in what we had to say, because he already knew the outcome, he already knew what we would say.

Can you now see something of the dilemma: if Jesus is really human, then when he asks us for advice he is really seeking help. Jesus is seeking help from us because he is searching for an answer, which is beyond his human ability. Is it possible that he could be seeking from us the wisdom of the word of God within us as a response to his questions?

If we hold to this image of Jesus, then understanding his words and actions as portrayed in the gospels requires a lot more explanation than a literal interpretation. How wonderful to begin to understand that Jesus was able to convey a wisdom and spiritual understanding of God and people, whilst being authentically human. It really means that it is possible for us who are wonderfully human to reach a similar understanding.

Having taken a step along this path, it is impossible now for me to turn back and accept the teaching of the past, even though the journey is not smooth, it is exciting. There have been times when I have experienced the God activity in my life and where there is no other explanation than to recognise the Spiritual influence of a loving God. These are the times that Marcus Borg calls the 'thin places' which are the places where we recognise the activity and presence of God. Not an 'elsewhere God' but a God who is present 'here and now'. Borg tells us that if we want to recognise the thin places, we must keep our 'hearts open'. A closed heart is insensitive to wonder, it affects the mind and the reasoning process. As Borg says, 'Blindness and limited vision go with a "closed heart", but most of all a closed heart forgets God; it does not allow for the "magic" around us to become reality.' Borg quotes Thomas Merton, the Trappist monk, in expressing his understanding of God:

> We are living in a world that is absolutely transparent, and God is shining through it all the time. This is not just a fable or a nice story. It is true. If we abandon ourselves to God and forget ourselves, we see it sometimes, and we see it maybe frequently. God shows himself everywhere in everything – in people and in things and in nature and events. It becomes very obvious that God is everywhere and in everything and we cannot be without him.

The Role of Faith Communities

Every now and then, we experience this God Spirit shining through. According to Borg, these are the 'thin places' where the veil momentarily lifts and we experience God. A thin place is anywhere where our hearts are open. It is the boundary between our world and the world of the Spirit. A thin place is a mediator of the sacred and this can appear to us in the shape of a stranger or friend, so keep your hearts and minds open, for even though the path may be bumpy, the experience of meeting God is mind blowing.

Progressive Jews have an expression I wish were ours – 'tikkun olam', which means literally 'repair of the world' through acts of kindness directed towards bringing this about. The world abounds with men and women, and young people especially these days, bent on 'tikkun olam' – Jewish or not, Christian or not. This is living evidence that whatever broke into history in the person of Jesus cannot be exterminated on a Roman cross. These people with their commitment to repair the world through kindness gives me a great sense of hope.

I have encountered many people who are continuing members of Christian communities and who have travelled a similar journey. In 2012, my colleague Rev. Rex Hunt and I co-edited a book entitled *New Life* – a collection of the life journeys of twenty-five laypeople and almost all recognised the need to challenge Christian orthodoxy including its doctrines, public worship, liturgies and everyday practical functioning. So how can we reshape our faith communities and reclaim the message of Jesus and his values for our world?

We can learn more from those considered to be the dregs of society, than the leaders of our faith community. Matthew also is alluding to the belief that the Jewish leaders of the day are hypocrites. Can these same accusations be levelled at us today?

Perhaps we need to ask ourselves the question, 'If the church as we know it ceased to exist, would God's work continue?' What is it that the church adds to our understanding of the society that makes for a better world?

These are the questions that we must honestly face and wrestle with if we are to be followers of Jesus of Nazareth rather than Jesus the Christ. Is it possible that by looking outside the square of traditional Christianity – that has in many ways restricted us – we just may find the true soul of God? How compelling to contemplate such a proposition, but also how challenging! Does the proposition of such an exploration quicken your pulse and speed your blood? As a result, are you beside yourself with joy?

OR... are you afraid of taking away something that is comfortable and secure, even if it is intellectually untenable?

Many who are travelling the progressive path are asking the question: 'Do established Christian communities live out in practice the values espoused by the historical Jesus?' And if they do, are they challenging the community when social evils such as those examined in chapter 6 arise and if they aren't what needs to change? To do this the future communities of faith need to change the language that Christian orthodoxy uses in public worship and we must remove all the hierarchical statements about the sacred energy we call God and revert to the message of Jesus.

The Role of Faith Communities

In an interview, Professor Lloyd Geering is quoted as saying that Jesus would be 'turning in his grave' if he heard that his followers were referring to him as 'King' or 'Lord'.

In a letter to *Crosslight* (the Uniting Church in Victoria's monthly newsletter) some years ago, Ian Cook took issue with these titles. He explains that it doesn't help us understand the person Jesus of Nazareth by referring to him as a king. In examining the role of kings in the last fifty years we see little of the Jesus-like figure. Ian suggested that the kings of today are all powerless, wealthy snobs, who are figureheads of elected governments. He raises the question that if Prince Charles ever became a king, would we look to him to gain insight into the person and nature of Jesus? He continues that he is also not happy with the title 'Lord' because it smacks of an elite group of privileged people from Europe such as the 'Lord of the manor'. Again stressing that these people are not exhibiting the behaviours we have come to expect of Jesus. Ian prefers to use such terms as 'friend' or 'servant' and I would add 'empowering companion', rather than Lord or King.

Over many years in ministry, my parishioners have raised this matter with me because they too were critical of these terms, because they understood Jesus to be a friend or humble servant committed to the equality and justice of all human beings. Then why has the church adopted the formal use of these terms, King, Lord, almighty?

Bishop Spong, through his fortnightly messages, has suggested that we often speak to God with the language of flattery, because we believe he will be influenced by this approach. It is assumed that if we continue to praise God with flowery language, he will protect us and answer our prayers. Often in public worship we give God titles such as 'Almighty', 'Ever Loving' and 'Eternal'. We also give God characteristics such as: 'You are more ready to hear than we are to pray' or 'your nature is to be merciful and long suffering'. Because flattery works with us, we assume it will work with God. A classic example is the hymn 'Immortal, Invisible, God only wise'. If we really believe that God can be swayed by flattery then what sort of vain God do we worship?

I would also suggest that matters such as 'papal infallibility' or 'scriptural inerrancy' are both patently absurd by any rational standard but they continue to be part of the security systems of competing religious traditions because they appeal to the human inability to cope with uncertainty. Is this why we use this language, not because it pleases God but, because it makes us feel comfortable and secure?

If we accept that the personally transforming power of Jesus comes from his ability to form close interpersonal relationships. then as followers of his way this is how we must respond to people we engage with. The questions that arise for many followers of the Galilean sage is, 'Does Christian orthodoxy follow this path?' and 'Does the current policy, practice and beliefs of orthodoxy encourage interpersonal supportive and growth-promoting relationships?' The Christian church to be true to its calling – must accept that we all 'belong to each other' and are 'responsible for each other'.

In an examination of the gospel narratives and the newly discovered sacred writings, we discover that Jesus has a

The Role of Faith Communities

belief in the inherent goodness of many of the people he encounters. However, what is it about Jesus that influences them? Is it only his words and his actions? As mentioned earlier, the Jesus Seminar writers in analysing the 'voiceprint' of Jesus and placing these words and actions in their historical matrix give us a glimpse of this historical figure. I would add that people were attracted to Jesus as a result of this, but even more so people are attracted to Jesus because he made them feel worthwhile, included and valued. He conveyed a passion about life that was empowering. He was able to convey that he understood how people felt when they were devalued or when they were excluded from community because of the laws associated with bodily functions that declared people unclean and unworthy to be embraced.

Did the words and actions of Jesus convey his emotions? When he cried at the death of a friend and when he reached out to touch people who were unclean and welcomed them with terms of endearment? Jesus made people aware of their worth by affirming that the spirit of sacred energy was within them and through recognising and drawing on this power they could accept themselves as whole in the eyes of God.

Relationships that value us as worthwhile human beings can bring us to a sense of wholeness. Perhaps the question we need to ask is not, 'What did we understand about the experience of an embracing relationship?' but, 'How did this relationship make us feel and did it change the way we behave?' By changing our image of ourselves we can embrace life with a passion and see the value in those we meet.

Chapter 9

Spirituality Without Borders

SPIRITUALITY IS OFTEN referred to as; 'The Spirit is life', 'ruah, breath, or wind'. To be spiritual is to be alive, filled with 'ruah', breathing deeply, and in touch with the wind. Spirituality is a life-filled path, a spirit-filled way of living. All who embark on a spiritual path need to be willing to learn and to let go: to know that none of us has all the answers and yet none of us is apart from divinity; to be able to let go of bitterness or prolonged anger. In his book *Creation Spirituality*, Matthew Fox writes, 'We must be emptied to walk down the pathway of spirituality, and of course the walk itself will accomplish its own surprising emptying'.

Many of those who have left the church fall into the category of what Bishop John Spong refers to as the 'Church Alumni' or the 'Believers in Exile', because many still hold that the basic teachings of Jesus of Nazareth and a metaphorical interpretation of the Bible stories have relevance to their life. Further, many would still claim a belief in a 'sacred life essence' and are more likely to refer to themselves as SBNR people - they are 'spiritual but not religious'. These people still affirm that one's spiritual task is to seek oneness with God, not some magical intervention by God.

If we are to follow the example of the historical Jesus, then we need to examine how Jesus understood the spiritual dimensions of his life and further how he continued to use the sacred spirit in his everyday living. In my many discussions with my friend Rev. Dr John Bodycomb, his biblical knowledge has provided me with a realistic and valuable insight into the daily spiritual practices of Jesus.

As a result of these discussions and the analysis of the writings of Matthew's Gospel, especially chapter 6, I now have come to the conclusion that contemplation and meditation on a daily basis are factors that influenced Jesus. In Matthew 6:6, we read these words 'But whenever you pray, go into your room and shut the door and pray to your Father who is in secret.' This verse says clearly to me that, for Jesus, real prayer was in essence an intensely private and individually personal matter.

It was John Bodycomb who informed me that in some of the twenty-five translations of this verse, eight say 'your room', five say 'inner room', four say 'closet', four have 'chamber', and two have 'inner chamber'. The original Greek word is *tameion* which can be translated as an 'inner' storage or chamber. My friend and colleague Dr Lorraine Parkinson says that because Jesus' spoken language is Aramaic, it is quite likely that he uses the word *tumaya* which can be interpreted as a 'secret place'.

These discussions have led me to believe that when Jesus uses the phrase 'go into your room', he is speaking metaphorically as he does in so many situations. I also believe that Jesus was a mystic and his contemplative approach to examining his approach to the world around him is the spirituality that he taught.

In his book *Adult Faith* (p. 105), Diarmuid O'Murchu lists eight defining characteristics of 'Adult Spirituality'. First, that the 'creative life force' we call God is to be recognised as being 'transpersonal', in that it not only embraces human personhood, but everything else in creation. This statement is also affirmed by Matthew Fox and those writers who support the concept of a 'spirituality' without borders, which is not determined only by religious believers, because love has no borders.

Secondly, adult spirituality seeks to engage with this great energy source of wisdom by adopting a 'multidisciplinary strategy' which includes the insights provided by science and cosmology.

Thirdly, the primary dynamic through which everything is developed and sustained is through our personal relationships.

Fourthly, adult spirituality encourages the seeking of truth through dialectics and lived experience, rather than relying on dogma, whether that is scientific or religious. It also views scripture as being culturally conditioned.

Fifthly, adult spirituality is committed to transformative living, as we are guided by the earth's wisdom. The choices we make through our commitment to contemplation, and the corresponding action we take, is aimed at ensuring that justice will prevail through mutual accountability.

Sixthly, spirituality seeks to honour our mortality in a finite world, as a paradox necessary for the creative freedom and flourishing of all earth's creatures.

The seventh characteristic of 'adult spirituality' is that while as humans we may accept the unique and important place we share in the realm of creation, we have no right of mastery or any form of domination, that could cause suffering for any of the 'Great Spirits' creation.

The eighth characteristic is that a key ingredient of any adult spirituality must accept and recognise the right of all of creation, in that humans have no special patriarchal control or right of domination over the earth's resources.

In my own personal life journey, I have come to learn that to live a 'good life' for me means to experience the sacred energy force I call God in the lives of those I meet. I needed to accept the events of life that my personal experience and reason explain for me, not what someone else describes for me be it a doctrine, creed or list of commandments.

In my teenage years, when I first came to identify myself as a friend of the historical Jesus and particularly his values, I became aware that the Jesus values that influenced me were not necessarily the values promulgated by orthodox Christianity, nor in fact were they the selfish values embraced by mainstream Western society. I found the values of Jesus more in line with the values my mother had taught me.

In the late 1980s, I came into contact with the writers of the Jesus Seminar – scholars such as Marcus Borg, John Dominic Crossan, Robert Funk and Bishop John Shelby

Spong to name a few. Their writings confirmed for me that the values of Jesus that I was committed to were most appropriate in living a 'good life'. This was particularly so when I saw myself as a Progressive Christian, which is one who is prepared to accept and embrace change and willing to work to reclaim the message of Jesus that is based on compassion, empathy and acceptance. A life that will take a stand against exclusion, hate, ignorance and violence.

As a Progressive Christian, I have become more concerned with life values as expressed in the life of Jesus, which I found in lives of people with whom I formed a close interpersonal relationship.

The consequence of this position means that – as a Uniting Church minister – I have now adopted a wisdom approach to religion. This means that I am concerned with relationships and how people can support each other, rather than embracing a 'priestly' religion which is more concerned about worship, and which is the approach expressed by Christian orthodoxy. As a consequence, I consider that the practice, structure and beliefs of Christian orthodoxy will not necessarily encourage an inclusive and caring community as envisioned by Jesus of Nazareth.

As recorded earlier, my personal moral coherence is grounded in my belief that every human being is precious and demanding of respect, and as human beings we depend on one another to survive and grow. Consequently, we are responsible to and for one another, and particularly to those who are most disadvantaged. The wellbeing of community and society as a whole depends on the quality of respect embodied in the interpersonal relationships between individuals, groups and the world we share. I affirm strongly that it is Jesus who has given us an example of how this can be achieved.

These conclusions have taken me many years of living experience to arrive at this point. They are supported by the highly acclaimed Australian social researcher Hugh Mackay in his book *The Good Life* where he states: 'The Good Life is not the sum of our security, wealth, status, postcode, career success and levels of happiness. The Good Life is one defined by our capacity for selflessness and our willingness to connect with others in a useful way'.

In her 2015 book *The Spiritual Child*, Dr Lisa Miller defines spirituality as 'an inner sense of relationship to a higher power that is loving and guiding'. Some may call this higher power God or nature, creator, or other words which infer the presence of a divine energy. The important point as emphasised by Dr Miller is that spirituality 'encompasses' a relationship and ability to communicate with this sacred energy.

The most important information provided by Dr Miller is that spirituality is an inborn fundamental to the human constitution, because spirituality connects brain, mind and body. Dr Miller also asserts that the natural spirituality with which we are born is closely allied with human bonding, creating relational spirituality, which is an experience of transcendence through relationships with one another, and with a higher energy source that as Jesus claims, is within ourselves. In the *Gospel of Mary* 4:5-7 we read, 'For the Child of Humanity is within you! Follow it! Those who seek it will find it. Go then and proclaim the good news of the realm'.

As a result of our biological wiring, we have an awareness of this transcendence, in us, around us, through us and beyond us, and it is this that makes us spiritual. It is transcendence that is more likely revealed in the positive emotions we bring to one another, such as compassion, empathy, unconditional love, forgiveness, hope and joy.

For followers of Jesus of Nazareth, the findings in this research by Dr Miller confirm the statements made by Jesus to his disciples, which states that the empowerment of God's spirit is present now within, between and around you. The conclusion of this research is that whenever we recognise this spiritual empowering influence, which is born in each of us, we must affirm it, whether it be in random acts of kindness, or in the generosity of spirit that we witness in the lives of people we come into contact with on a daily basis. Because to know God's power in the way that Jesus knew it, is to know the empowering energy of God as a practical reality.

As a result of my own personal experience, I see my role now as a committed subversive saboteur, with the aim of rescuing the message of the human Jesus from the distorted view of both orthodox Christianity and mainstream Western society. It is by emphasising the alternative practical wisdom of Jesus with his commitment to the importance of personal relationships of quality and respect, that I strongly believe we will then be able to embrace the value of gracious compassionate living with the sacred source of love.

Unfortunately, many world leaders do not appear to hold these values. For example, politics in the United States of America encourages the importance of individualism, tribalism, patriotism and nationalism over community wellbeing and the good of all humanity. The Trump administration is a classic example, because it strongly supports patriotism even to the point that they are prepared to enter into military conflict with other nations to achieve this.

Recently in Australia, under the Morrison Government, we are witnessing a similar political approach especially when it comes to border protection against refugees seeking asylum. On 3 October 2019, the Prime Minister Scott Morrison delivered a lecture to the Lowy Institute outlining his vision for Australia's role in relation to what he termed 'Globalism'. As the Rev. Dr Noel Preston wrote in his response to this paper, 'the conclusions presented by the Prime Minister are disturbing for many Australians of goodwill, who are seeking a better approach by our nation as an international citizen in honouring our commitment to the values of the United Nations'.

The Prime Minister's paper clearly calls on Australians to ignore their responsibility to be less self-centred. There was no mention by him about our global responsibility to 'climate change' or the government's record of all persuasions on matters such as the diminishing humanitarian overseas aid and the cruelty of Australia's approach to border control. These political approaches are based on the illusion that some people are of more value than others.

Spiritually, there are growing numbers of people who previously identified themselves as Christians who are now moving away from defining themselves by lists of beliefs and toward a practical way of life primarily defined by the power of love. These are people who are increasingly rejecting the image of the sacred source of energy most call God as one who has been depicted as an interventionist, violent and judgmental Supreme Being. They are now seeking to understand their life through the embrace of a renewing natural spirit already at work in our world. These are people who are joining with people of other faiths and those with no faith at all to dedicate themselves to loving and healing the earth and to building peace through active cooperation. Together they seek to overcome injustice, poverty, and racism to create a more egalitarian future for all.

If God is the universal and inward impulse that inspires us to seek the best for others and the growth of the beloved, then when we have learned to do that for ourselves, we will have evolved to a fuller awareness of our spiritual energy, and God may well have worked herself out of a job.

Reaching our ability to form and maintain positive growth-promoting relationships is an evolutionary process that only comes from continuous practice. And as Joe Bessler writes in *The Historical Jesus Goes to Church*, the best place to practise this is with faith communities that share a belief in the optimism of spirituality.

A fuller humanity means we need look no further for a sacred energy than to find within us the face of God. When we recognise that we are a community, not merely a collection of self-interested individuals then justice, integrity and trust in fundamental institutions are essential social assets, and social capital is as important as economic prosperity.

This approach to living by the values of Jesus raises for us many unanswered questions, for example where do we stand in relation to capital punishment? Should drug dealers be executed? Do we believe that all life comes from God and is sacred? Where do we stand on this religious and political issue? Are we afraid to support the rights of disadvantaged people, because we will be called too political?

Does the Church have an advocacy role? Does it have a prophetic role? Should we as a body of believers be seeking to have an enlightened debate, which is followed by positive action on the human impact of global warming?

I am sure most people will agree that as individuals and corporately as the church, we have a role to play in standing in solidarity with the marginalised, the demonised and the disadvantaged. We also have a role in ensuring that we do all that is in our power to save the planet from irreparable harm for future generations.

No one is suggesting that we can say the government is doing all it can. No one is saying we should bury our heads in the sand and hope these problems will go away. So what is our role?

Like religions and faiths, no single political party or system has all the answers. The governments in Australia are elected in most instances by the majority of the voters, although there have been instances such as the 2001 Federal election when this was not the case. However, if governments are elected by the majority. they are also responsible to the majority and not just to vested interests.

This simply means that we, as followers of Jesus, have a responsibility to ensure that the values that we hold dear, the values that we find in the life of Jesus of Nazareth, will guide our deliberations and encourage us to make them known particularly on social justice issues.

No political party in Australia – and I cannot say this strongly enough – can deliver this and no political party has a monopoly on values and morals. At the funeral of the wife of a Labor minister during the Hawke Government, I was pleased to witness that it was a Liberal colleague who was the first to embrace the grieving husband. It was positive to see that compassion was seen as more important than political belief.

The principle behind our actions must be related to how we understand our faith not simply what others say to us, be they politicians; be they civic or religious leaders. The decision is ours to make. It is in God that we live and breathe and have our being, not political systems. It is the compassion of Jesus and his actions that challenges us about our involvement in the life around us.

For these reasons, I will continue to raise issues of social justice in my role as a minister of the Uniting Church and I will continue to urge the church to make a stand where people are victimised, maligned and mistreated. If this is political, then so be it, but no political party should be free from our criticisms.

By offering the alternative wisdom of Jesus the Galilean sage, with his commitment to the importance of personal relationships of quality, we are able embrace the value of gracious living rather than an adherence to a dogmatic belief.

Chapter 10

'Our Role in Community as Subversives'

WHAT IS THE ROLE OF subversive communities in following the way of Jesus of Nazareth? According to Marcus Borg, for Jesus the pathway for a personal transformation to wholeness was firmly grounded in a subversive wisdom.

Rev. John Cranmer's poem 'Subverting your World with a Handful of Stories' expresses it:

> The telling of stories
> is at the heart of making a new world
> they have inherent within them
> seeds of many possible futures
> they take root in the most rocky of soils
> and surprising places of uncertainty
> creating strongly blooming imaginations
> that have decided to live forever.
> (Used by permission).

Those who believe there is a right and wrong time and place to protest against injustices are those whose privilege protects them from the social injustices that prevail in our community. Those who are prepared, with Rev. Dr Martin Luther King, Jr, to live by the principle that the right time to do the right thing is now, privileged or not, remind us of the immorality of acquiescence, apathy, indifference, denial, negligence, and procrastination in confronting injustice and evil.

What we need to believe, and teach our children to believe, is that there is never a wrong time or wrong place to oppose injustice. The time is always now to oppose injustice and promote the equality of worth for all peoples.

As Dr King has stated: 'In the Beloved Community, poverty, hunger, and homelessness will not be tolerated because international standards of human decency will not allow it. Racism and all forms of discrimination, bigotry, and prejudice will be replaced by an all-inclusive spirit of sisterhood and brotherhood.'

Rev. Bret Myers stated in 2017 in an article 'Right and Wrong Times and Places' for *ProgressiveChristianity.org*, 'To refuse to be brave for the sake of others is to live a selfish life which promotes the values of safety, comfort, and security above compassion, peace, and justice. It is to value power over freedom and injustice over equality'.

Bret later explained: 'I'd rather die at the hands of oppressors than live in the complacency of watching others denied the very rights I get to take for granted. Both lifestyles reflect a certain kind of character, but only the former is based in ethical integrity and is one that I can admire and respect'.

Bret also states that the promoting of compassion is an extension of the 'Golden Rule' when he raises the question, 'Is this not what the founders of the world's religions taught us? Is it not the Golden Rule? To risk danger to oneself for the sake of another is to love, as we want to be loved. Wishing others well while refusing to help is not what we'd respect in others, so how can we respect such behaviour in ourselves?'

Hence, as Bret claims, 'Our virtues and core values have to apply at all times and all places, else they are not really our virtues and values. Integrity is not conditional, and decency is not whimsical'.

As Martin Luther King stated: 'Now is always the time to act on behalf of those suffering from injustices, for now is when we want them to act on our behalf if the situation was reversed'.

In our current global economic situation, I am reminded of the story in Matthew 22:20-21 where Jesus is questioned about the right to pay tax or not. Remember, he is given a coin, which is an indication that he did not have one on him, and he asks whose head is on the coin. When those present reply 'the emperor's', he replies, 'Give to the emperor what is his and to God what is God's'.

This gospel story – as with most – lends itself to being acted out rather than read as a record of dialogue, because only when we actually live out the story can it come alive. Jesus' retort to the students who attempt to trap him is a masterful piece of repartee. He avoids being ensnared by the question without really solving the issue; he doesn't advise them to pay the tax and he doesn't advise them not to pay it. He does advise them to know the difference between the claims of the emperor and the claims of God.

The Pharisees and the Sadducees were continually challenging Jesus about matters of law because many laws bound the Jews; in fact there were 613 different commandments in Judaism at the time of Jesus. Of these, 365 were negative commands beginning with 'you shalt not' and 248 with 'you shall'. The Pharisees were skilled at interpreting the law but, in this case, they sent their students. They did not risk going themselves because, if their trap succeeded, they could not be blamed whereas if their trap failed they would not be ridiculed.

They instructed their students on the question to ask, with the aim of trapping Jesus because this was clearly a dilemma for whatever answer Jesus gives could be used against him.

To understand the significance of this dilemma, we need to understand the makeup of the population of Palestine of those days because it was not a simple society of peasant farmers, artisans and fishermen, as I used to imagine. By 63 BC, the Romans had colonised Palestine and in accordance with their policy of appointing native rulers they eventually made Herod the king of the Jews. In Jesus' time, Herod the Great died and his kingdom was divided up. However, there was rebellion to this authority brought on to some extent by the weakness of the leaders appointed by the Romans, but due primarily to the issue of taxation.

The Jews objected on religious grounds to paying the tax and rose up in rebellion. The leader of this rebellion

'Our Role in Community as Subversives'

was Judas the Galilean, who founded a religiously inspired movement of freedom fighters called Zealots. The Roman response was to crucify two thousand of them. The Zealots were an underground group of rebels loosely organised but, as a result of the Roman resistance, they became organised, and for 60 years they harassed the Roman army. The last group held out at the fortress of Masada until 73 CE when nearly a thousand of them chose to commit suicide rather than surrender to the Romans. The Zealots were faithful Jews, zealous for the law and for the sovereignty and kingship of God.

Another important group operating at this time were the Pharisees. They paid their taxes to Rome but did so under protest. They separated themselves from others whom they considered not faithful to the law and traditions. Their name means 'the separate ones'. They believed in an after-life, in the resurrection of the dead and in a future Messiah whom God would send to liberate them from the Romans.

A third group, the Essenes, went even further than the Pharisees in striving for perfection. They separated themselves completely and led a celibate life in camps in the desert. This separation and commitment to the rites of purification was done because they believed the end of the world was near. They were just as warlike as the Zealots but they did not think that the time was right for rebellion. It is possible that John the Baptist was an Essene; however, he broke with their tradition when he offered baptism to all comers.

Then there were the Sadducees. They were the conservatives who clung to the ancient Hebrew traditions. Rewards and punishment were to be found in this life. They collaborated with the Romans and endeavoured to maintain the status quo. The Sadducees also included the scribes who were lawyers, teachers and men of learning. They were often from the landed aristocracy and seen as the leaders of the people. They did not believe in an afterlife, but they believed that reward and punishment was found in this life.

This is the scene in which Jesus enters, not the quiet country life we may have imagined. Add to this the fact that Jesus was himself a fugitive after his confrontation in the temple with the moneychangers.

Jesus sets out to liberate Israel from Rome but not as the Zealots do; he wants to do this by persuading Israel to change. Without a change in heart within Israel itself, liberation of any kind would not be possible. As Jesus saw it, the only way to be liberated from your enemies was to love them, to do good to those who hate you and to pray for those who treat you badly.

This does not mean that you resign yourself to the oppression, nor is it a matter of killing people with kindness. It is a matter of reaching down to the root cause of oppression and domination: which is humanity's lack of compassion. The Jews could overthrow the Romans, but if they still lacked compassion, they would not be liberated.

The Zealots wanted a mere change of government from Roman to Jewish. Jesus wanted a change that would affect every department of life; he wanted a qualitatively different world. Jesus saw what no one else was able to see that there was more exploitation and domination from within Judaism than there was without. The people had to suffer

'Our Role in Community as Subversives'

more oppression at the hands of the Sadducees, Pharisees, Scribes and Zealots than on account of the Romans. The protest against Roman oppression was hypocritical and this is the very point that Jesus makes in the gospel reading, 'Give to Caesar what is Caesar's and to God what is God's'.

This response amazed the Pharisees who did not have a counter response. However, this statement, when teased out, raises more questions especially for modern day followers of this Galilean sage. For example, how do we determine what belongs to God and what belongs to the political authorities?

Does obedience to the values of Jesus today bring us into conflict with values or lack of values of the current political authorities? When does the authority of the state overrule our belief in the values of Jesus?

In today's world, when political authorities are primarily concerned with personal power and refuse to accept their responsibility for the care of our environment and the support of people in need, this question of Jesus is vital. Further, how do we respond to the government's lack of compassion for refugees and asylum seekers or their encouragement of racial vilification in the name of 'free speech'?

When we examine the gospel stories of Jesus, it is abundantly clear that Jesus is a revolutionary figure and as such is a deep threat to the political powers of the day. His values are clearly those of a compassionate egalitarian figure, whether it is about economic equality, racism, or the rights of women.

Jesus' answer reveals not only the hypocrisy and insincerity of the question but also the real motive behind the taxation issue, namely greed for money. The people who ask the question are in possession of Roman coins, coins that were seen as the personal property of the ruler who issued them. It is not God's money but Caesar's; if you refuse to give it back to him, it can only be because you are a lover of money. If you really wished to give to God what belonged to God, then you would sell your possessions and give to the poor, and you would give up your desire for power prestige and possessions.

The real issue was oppression itself not the fact that a pagan Roman dared to oppress God's chosen people. The root cause of oppression was humanity's lack of compassion. Those who resented Roman oppression but overlooked their own oppression of the poor were lacking in compassion as much, if not more so, than the Romans.

The struggles of the Zealots had nothing whatsoever to do with genuine liberation. They were fighting for Jewish nationalism, Jewish racialism, Jewish superiority and Jewish prejudice.

True liberation means taking up the cause of people as human beings. To love your enemy is to live in solidarity with all people. The revolution that Jesus wanted to bring about was far more radical than anything the Zealots or anyone else may have had in mind.

Every sphere of life – political, economic, social and religious –was radically questioned by Jesus and turned upside down. In all of the parables, Jesus emphasises the God of compassion, rather than the God of holiness and his criticism of the Zealots is not because they were too political; his criticism – as with the Pharisees and the Essenes – is

'Our Role in Community as Subversives'

that they are too religious and this was a loveless religion. What led the Pharisees to oppress the poor and the Zealots to assassinate fellow Jews who betrayed them, was their religious fanaticism.

One of the most significant causes of oppression, discrimination and suffering in that society was religion – the loveless religion of religious fanatics – the religion of human beings.

Without compassion, religious beliefs are useless and empty; without compassion, all politics will be oppressive, even the politics of revolution.

Surely, the most surprising thing in the gospels is that Jesus preached about a religious-political 'kingdom' from which the religious of the day were excluded or rather from which they would exclude themselves. According to Matthew, Jesus told them that the tax collectors and the prostitutes are making their way into the kingdom of God and not you.

It would have been impossible for the religious people of Jesus' time to see him as a religious person. They would have seen him as a blasphemously irreligious man who under the cloak of religion was undermining all the values upon which religion, politics, economics and society were based. He was a dangerous, subversive revolutionary who must be done away with, and that is exactly what happened because they couldn't cope with the truth of his message.

A question that those who follow the way of the Galilean sage need to ask is, 'Did Jesus at anytime show annoyance or anger when he was faced with an injustice and if he did what form did it take?

John W. H. Smith

In Matthew 21:12-17, we read that Jesus, while in the Temple, overturned the tables of the 'money changers' because he claimed that it is written that, 'My house shall be called a house of prayer but you are making it a den of robbers'. It appears that by turning over the tables, Jesus is displaying a righteous anger at the money changers because they are misusing the Temple. This is an example of righteous anger because it is in this context of constructive activism that we associate the activities of people such as Mahatma Ghandi and Rev. Dr Martin Luther King.

In this example, we have the historical Jesus confronting injustice in a non-violent revolutionary manner. In his book *Jesus and Nonviolence: A Third Way*, the scholar Walter Wink explains that, while Jesus' actions were non-violent, they were not passive resistance either but active non-violent resistance, because not aimed at humiliating, dominating or controlling.

Righteous anger reveals to us the faces of the damned and those who are rejected and disrespected. For Martin Luther King, the overturning of the tables by Jesus and the fighting against the forces of injustice gave rise to King's concept of the 'beloved community' because God is love and love demands justice.

In today's world there will be times – be it the abuse of children or the disregard of the rights of women and people with different views of sexual orientation – which will cause us as friends of Jesus to overturn the tables and to stand beside those who have been treated unjustly.

'Our Role in Community as Subversives'

Let us give thanks to this God of Jesus who challenges us to get our priorities right, where we can put compassion before power, profit and religious zeal.

However, the statement by Jesus regarding paying tax to Caesar, when teased out, raises more questions especially for modern day followers of this Galilean sage. For example, how do we determine what belongs to God and what belongs to the political authorities? Does obedience to the values of Jesus bring us into conflict with values or lack of values of current political authorities? When does the power of the state overrule our belief in the values of Jesus? Most importantly of all, what should be our reaction?

In today's world when political authorities are primarily concerned with personal power and refuse to accept their responsibility for the care of our environment, this question of Jesus in vital. Further how should we respond to the government's lack of compassion for refugees and asylum seekers or the encouragement of racial vilification in the name of 'free Speech'?

As Robin Meyers clearly declares in his book *Spiritual Defiance*, 2015, p. xiii, 'whatever else may be said of the Jesus movement, it was born in opposition to the status quo. Its founder constituted an unacceptable risk to the Roman Empire, and this resistance was seen as counter-intuitive and subversive'.

When we examine the gospel stories of Jesus, it is abundantly clear that Jesus is a revolutionary figure and as such is a deep threat to the political powers of the day. His values are clearly those of a compassionate egalitarian figure, whether it is about equality, racism, or the rights of women.

The values of Jesus lead us to re-think the way we live in community and in the wider community. While the empires of our day – like that of Rome in the time of Jesus – believe that peace can only be achieved through victory, Jesus' values show us a different way that peace will only be achieved in when all people experience justice. If the world could be governed by the same values that good friends share, there would be peace.

When I identify myself as a friend of Jesus, I am aware that the values I hold are not those promulgated by 'orthodox Christianity' nor in fact are they the values of mainstream Western society.

As a progressive Christian who identifies with the 'historical Jesus', I have become more concerned about life values than rigid religious doctrines, creeds and beliefs. As a result, my values are now in conflict with values of mainstream western civilization and Christian orthodoxy. The current crisis facing our world in the twenty-first century is not the work of the sacred energy source we call God. It is the work of the 'Empire', be it Rome, be it Western civilization, be it Christian orthodoxy.

The consequence of this position means that I now embrace a 'wisdom' approach to living rather than a 'priestly' or 'prophetic' position, which the Christian orthodoxy embraces. Further, I believe that the practice, structure and beliefs of Christian orthodoxy will not encourage an inclusive and caring community as envisioned by Jesus. These conclusions have taken many years of living

'Our Role in Community as Subversives'

experience to reach this point. As a result, I see my role now as a subversive saboteur with the aim of rescuing the message of the human Jesus from the distorted view of both orthodox Christianity and mainstream Western society.

This liberation movement is aimed not only at liberating people controlled by internal and external forces, but to ensure that the Spirit of Jesus our founder is also liberated so it can be a continuing influence in the world and importantly not controlled by any one person or body. There will be times if we are defending the rights of people against injustice that, like Jesus, we will need to break the laws of the state and of the church.

So often we hear Christian church leaders and state and national politicians falsely claiming allegiance to the Spirit of Jesus by calling themselves Christian, but they are proclaiming their own message about Jesus, rather than his message about living graciously with a commitment to social justice for all people. These leaders, by their actions and words, have demonstrated that they are morally incoherent, because they are more concerned with gaining personal power than empowering others. It is their actions that belie their words. The true spirit of the Jesus message must be once again established in the community.

For many years, my mother persistently encouraged me to believe that the world in which I lived could be a better place, and she subjected me to an initial grooming for this role. She encouraged me to believe that all people should be afforded the opportunity to develop their full potential, and that it was possible to establish a more socially just and financially equitable society. Further, she insisted that we could not leave these tasks to others, because we all had a responsibility to ensure these were not simply hollow words, but through our own endeavours we could make this a living reality.

I am now aware that even as a small child my thoughts and actions were being formed by my mother who encouraged me to look for the best in people and to do whatever I could to help them to achieve their full potential. She also encouraged me to read the subversive literature of Hugo, Tolstoy and Dostoevsky. However, the impact of this influence only became significant when, at the age of sixteen, I came in contact with the Methodist Church through the influence of friends. It was here that my mother's grooming in my early years began to blossom.

It was when I came back into the formal church in my teenage years that I began to understand Jesus as a rebellious leader who was challenging the authority of both the church and government of his day by providing support for those people who had been disadvantaged by the religious and political systems of the day.

In these early days of my attachment to the church, I remember finding a number of 'left wing' 'Wanted' posters of Jesus. These posters referred to Jesus as a subversive and that he was 'Wanted' by the authorities for a conspiracy to overthrow the government. Jesus was also accused on these posters for practising medicine without a licence as well as illegally healing on the Sabbath. He was also accused of consorting with Gentiles and sending revolutionaries out into the world to convey his egalitarian message of a loving God.

'Our Role in Community as Subversives'

These claims meant that Jesus was considered an enemy of the state by consorting with radicals, prostitutes, dissidents and the poor. It was also claimed that he had embarked on a criminal career when he announced public insults by calling Herod a 'fox' (Luke 13:32) and comparing Rabbis with John the Baptist as 'reeds blowing in the wind' (Matthew 11:7). This inferred that they were swayed this way and that by the winds of popular opinion rather than defending the rights of those in need. Jesus knew that a reed trembling in the wind was the opposite to John's character because John was prepared to defend his integrity even when it meant placing his life at risk.

The church authorities of the day condemned him also for violating the rights of the Temple by offering forgiveness and fellowship with God to sinners because this violated the Temple monopoly of public expiation and forgiveness. The posters also claimed that he cleverly disguised his anti-government propaganda in the form of coded answers and confusing aphorisms and, by so doing, Jesus was able to gather a following of people who believed and accepted these treasonable comments.

It is interesting to note that these posters about the 'subversive' Jesus became available to the church communities before the books from the Jesus Seminar scholars had been published. The writings of these scholars supported the subversive approach of the historical Jesus.

On reading these posters, I found a Jesus I could embrace primarily as a result of my early childhood which was influenced by the values of my mother. However, when I raised these issues with the lay people of my congregation,

I was firmly warned that these posters did not reflect the person of Jesus that the church believed in. I remember being informed by a number of lay people that God ordained our 'Royal' and 'political' leaders and as a result we must obey them even, if it meant that many people were suffering injustice as a result of their activities. This advice flew in the face of my understanding of Jesus' message.

However, I found support for my belief that these posters reflected the true Jesus of history in a number of Methodist clergy who encouraged me to continue with my search for the real Jesus. My mentors at this time were the Rev. Norman Paske, Rev. Alf Foote, Rev. Andrew McCutcheon, Rev. John Westerman, and particularly the Rev. Dudley Hyde who shared his concerns regarding Christian orthodoxy's lack of understanding of the importance of the historical Jesus in his book, *Rescuing Jesus: A Heretic Handbook*.

These mentors supported me by suggesting that I should continue to belong to the organised church and even to accept a full time working arrangement by becoming ordained. It was also made abundantly clear that I should not allow myself to be seduced by the orthodox approach of the Christian Church, but that I should remain true to my commitment to the revolutionary message of the rebellious Jesus. To maintain my true mission goals I needed to continue to remain in the church, so as to prevent my belief in the subversive Jesus from being undermined.

In the life I have left to me, I wish to continue the task I believe I have been given, which is to smuggle the true Jesus back into the Christian Community and into everyday living, against all opposition.

'Our Role in Community as Subversives'

In the person of Jesus, I have discovered a human being who has a faith and belief in the inherent goodness of common humanity, and who seeks to offer the opportunity for all people to be liberated from the fears and restrictions placed upon them by the structures of society and their own feelings of insecurity, even if this means being labelled a subversive. Our founder, the sage, Jesus of Nazareth, has also alerted us of the danger to civil liberties by a hierarchical religion and a power-obsessed, brutal government.

My role over the years has undergone a process of refinement but the revolutionary zeal still remains. My mother's encouragement to be an agent of change is, I believe, stronger today than at any other time in my life. I have tried to assist the people I meet to personally discern that they have the ability to reach a sense of wholeness of being, by recognising the power that resides within them, which is the same Spirit experienced by the founder of our revolutionary movement, the sage Jesus of Nazareth.

I was carefully taught by my mentors that the best modus operandi was to alert people to the fact that the power to change was within them, in much the same way that the founder of our revolutionary movement had been able to effect change: this indwelling power, he claims, is connected by a spiritual force to the great energy of the universe.

This energy becomes visible not only through the words and actions of people operating in normal everyday situations but often in a subversive way such as through humour, wit, sarcasm or exaggeration. Many people who became influential in this movement are unaware that they had become instruments of the revolution. Some of the greatest exponents of liberation would not be able to raise to consciousness the reasons for their behaviour, which in no way demeans their efforts.

Jesus' belief in the inherent goodness of the people he meets comes from his belief that the sacred energy source we call God is within each person and it comes to visibility primarily in the way we relate personally to each other. Subversives recognise that the greatest weapon that will effect meaningful change is to speak the truth as they understand it.

Speaking the truth in defence of other humans can cause societal rejection, especially when powerful government bodies orchestrate this rejection. For example, in the United States of America, a singing group the 'Dixie Chicks' who are a prolific American country music band from Texas have experienced this rejection when they spoke the truth, as they understood it. In March 2003, whilst performing at a London concert just days prior to the American invasion of Iraq, the lead singer Natalie Maines announced to the audience; 'Just so you know, we don't want this war, this violence, and we are ashamed that the president of the United States, (George W Bush) is from Texas'.

As a result of this public statement, there was an affirmative reaction in England; however, in the USA, there was a strong negative response from talk show hosts who publicly denounced them. There were public demonstrations of people destroying their records. This led to their popularity plummeting out of the bestseller lists. Further, many media networks for the rest of Bush's presidency blacklisted them.

'Our Role in Community as Subversives'

In the months following their return to the US, they received numerous death threats. In an attempt to emotionally come to terms with this violent reaction, they decided to write a song about the impact of this experience. In March 2006, they released their cathartic response to their experience in the song, 'Not Ready To Make Nice'. The lyrics powerfully express the emotions they were all experiencing as a result of the violent response they had received and is captured in the following words:

> It's a sad, sad story
> When a mother will teach her daughter
> That she ought to hate a perfect stranger
> And how in the world
> Can the words that I said
>
> Send somebody so over the edge
> That they'd write me a letter
> Saying that I better Shut up and sing
> Or my life will be over?
>
> I'm not ready to make nice
> I'm not ready to back down.

It was just not the violent invasion of a sovereign country that this group alone protested about, because in 2005 along with thirty-one well-known recording artists including such people as Dolly Parton that a record was released supporting relationships of all kinds, regardless of sexual orientation or gender identity, called 'I Believe in Love'.

It is important to note that at this time a majority of the Christian orthodox communities along with many high profile politicians refused to support the call for justice and equal rights in the LGBTQI community. The reaction of major entertainment companies for exercising their right of free speech blacklisted the Dixie Chicks along with other courageous entertainers. Their response clearly demonstrates the level of irrational fear that continues to pervade modern society toward those who dare to be different and who are willing to speak the truth, as they understand it.

Non-violent strategist Gene Sharp wrote, 'A closer examination of the sources of the rulers' power indicates that they depend intimately upon the obedience and cooperation of the governed'. When we increase the visibility of Christians taking risks, it encourages others to take risks, significantly increasing the pressure on a government that is not delivering positive outcomes for society. Increasing visible risks uses the intangible power of traditional religious values and morality to undermine key sources of power for authority. In the case of challenging family separation and child detention, taking increased risks to say 'no' to these policies creates a fertile ground for the conditions to change.

As Mexican Gandhian strategist and Catholic Pietro Ameglio puts it, 'When laws become so egregious that life and creation are at risk, then the moral imperative is clear: Disobedience in the face of what is inhuman is a personal, religious, and social virtue to increase the good'. Or as proposed by Rose Marie Berger, 'Disobedience in the face of what is inhuman is a personal, religious, and social virtue to increase the good'.

'When Injustice is Enshrined in Law, Defiance becomes Essential.' This was a painted sign I discovered on a wall in the inner city suburb of Brunswick, Victoria, which appealed to me because it supports those who are experiencing the agony of injustice committed by government authorities. Perhaps Simon and Garfunkel were correct when they wrote, 'The words of the prophets are written on the subway walls, tenement halls'.

When we reclaim the message of Jesus that the sacred energy we call God is within us and we accept the 'historical Jesus rather than the Christ of the church, we are correctly referred to by church authorities as 'heretics'. If we reclaim the message of Jesus, which is in conflict with the theology of orthodoxy, because the way of Jesus is to oppose elitism, then yes, we need to accept that we are heretics but, in the words of my colleague Rev. Dr John Bodycomb, we need to be 'heretics with a passion'. He wrote this in an unpublished manuscript called *Heretics Ablaze* where he calls on heretics to stand tall in defence of the truth of the historical Jesus of Nazareth.

The relevant questions regarding the value of 'Spiritual Defiance', raised by Robin Meyers 2015 (xvii) are, 'Where are the Holy Fools for God today? Who stands out in the crowd as a troublemaker for justice? Where can we find the spiritual contrarian, unplugged and unmoved by the choreographed hysteria of celebrity culture? Where do we find real wisdom in the age of the blog, where everyone with an opinion can self publish, where authors presume not to need editors in a worldwide web of intellectual autoeroticism?'

Chapter 11
The Future Structure of Inclusive Faith Communities

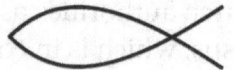

ROBERT MILLER FINDS THE PROBLEMS of the imperial structure of orthodox Christianity in Joe Bessler's article 'Facing Hard Questions' p. 47 of *The Future of the Christian Tradition*. In this article, Bessler claims that for more than 200 years, Christian theologians, clergy and community leaders have failed in explaining to their communities the challenge created by a scientific understanding of reality. In most situations, they have simply chosen to ignore this challenge. Instead, they purposely fostered a subservient approach to hierarchical authorities, instead of encouraging and nurturing a search into the intellectual and moral complexities of living in the twenty-first century. They have continued to propound a significantly narrow 'spirituality', based upon the narrow teachings of so-called infallible Scripture or infallible teachers.

The Future Structure of Inclusive Faith Communities

They have aligned the Christian church to the structural systemic approach of imperial powers, which includes its elitism and violence towards those who questioned these beliefs. Orthodoxy has failed and neo-orthodoxy is on the same path if it refuses to ask the moral and ethical questions that affect all people in the twenty-first century. More than this the future of 'faith communities' will be determined by their actions based on their ethics. They will be regarded not for what they say, but what they do and how they live. Hence there is an urgent need to redefine the role of Jesus' message through alternative structures.

My understanding of the divine presence that I call God comes from the continuous interplay of the five influences propounded by John Wesley. By this I mean that if there is a conflict between 'scripture' and 'experience' or 'scripture' and 'knowledge', I need to review my original orthodox understanding of the scriptural base. The same can be said when 'knowledge' or 'scripture' conflicts with 'tradition'.

For example, if 'reason' as a result of personal 'experience' is in conflict with a scriptural interpretation regarding the 'nature miracles', how then do we interpret their meaning? In later years, I have relied more on 'metaphor' and 'midrash' than on literal interpretation.

This has been a major task for my spiritual journey in the last twenty years, as New Testament scholarship, particularly around the 'historical Jesus' has increased. Writers/scholars such Crossan, Borg, Funk, Miller, Brandon Scott, Karen Armstrong and Stephen Patterson have had a profound influence on my understanding of the New Testament. The translations of ancient documents found at Nag Hammadi and in particular the Gnostic gospels, have also raised questions for my journey.

The book *A New New Testament*, edited by Professor Hal Taussig, is a carefully documented gathering of sacred texts discovered at Nag Hammadi. He brought together a Council of Scholars to examine these sacred texts, and they have added a further ten volumes to the books already included in the Bible. Among them are *The Gospel of Thomas, The Gospel of Truth, The Acts of Paul and Thecla* and *The Gospel of Mary*.

Some of these texts had been lost or mislaid. Others, such as *The Acts of Paul and Thecla*, written in the late first or early second century, were never lost. By the second century, this text was extremely popular, as was the person of Thecla herself. She had the following of a modern day movie star. Unfortunately, her popularity was criticised by the early church fathers such as Tertullian, as was her self-baptism after Paul refused to baptise her. This could have been a major reason for the text not to be included in the Bible, if it was seen as being critical of the apostle Paul.

The great value of Taussig's latest book is that, by adding these additional sacred texts to the range and depth of the early sacred writers in one volume, it allows for an informed, comparative analysis.

Importantly, this innovative work is written in twenty-first century with easy to read language, which will encourage in its readers to explore a deepening spiritual awareness.

You may ask, why has Professor Taussig been so well received? The answer is his ability to communicate complex messages in easy to listen to language. Whether reading his texts or listening to his presentations, you will feel engaged with the message.

He is a great storyteller because as, he is revealing his story, he is also communicating wisdom, which at times can be quite unconventional. His stories are often embedded in our history and are substantiated by Taussig with clear documented evidence. Perhaps the reason Progressive Christianity has been so widely embraced by people from all walks of life is a direct result of the influence of people like Taussig and their ability to communicate complex issues in everyday language.

As a result of the information in these new sacred texts and in particular the *Gospels of Thomas, Mary*, and *Truth*, all of which support strongly the message of Jesus, as opposed to the message of Christian orthodoxy. I am more profoundly spiritual now than at any time in my life as a result of these new sacred texts. I may still challenge the truth of creeds, but not the need to affirm the presence of God's reign within. My experience of the cosmic spirit of God as a loving force may conflict with the doctrine of the atonement, but it doesn't threaten my faith in God.

I am interested in and enjoy the company of people particularly when we are discussing personal issues, because I am seeking always to develop personal and enduring relationships. I am very enthusiastic about the joy of life and want to share my understanding of the presence of the divine with others. Not with the aim of convincing them, but to encourage them to express their own understanding. Sharing ideas and beliefs successfully requires one to be a good teacher and communicator. I believe I am able to encourage others to explore their potential because I consider myself to be a participant leader, so at times there will be a need to express one's understanding of the truth, but this can only be done with a deep sensitivity to the needs of others.

Nurturing the strengths of its members and encouraging the development of mutually beneficial relationships with all its members best serve a congregation/community of faith. Only then can we truly stand in solidarity with other human beings and share our journey with those outside the community. For me, this is possible by following the way of Jesus of Nazareth who reveals in his words and actions the reality of the sacred in the lives of those he encounters.

Biblical religion can be expressed in at least three ways, the way of the priest, the way of the prophet and the way of wisdom. The priestly religion is about worship and authority and it is dominated by rules, ritual, doctrines and creeds. Unfortunately the commitment to these activities will at times become more important than the way we relate to each other.

In the 'priestly religion', the community of faith hand over the authority and responsibility for its life to paid clergy who are given power by virtue of their ordination and induction by the church authorities. The priestly approach aspires to the sublime but rarely rises above some ritual form. Some people have irreverently referred to the priestly approach as being simply concerned with the 'smells, bells and whistles'. The orthodox Christian church, in the main, supports priestly religion; unfortunately, quite often, it is the priests and clergy who become the 'gatekeepers' of our faith.

The Future Structure of Inclusive Faith Communities

The second approach is that of 'prophetic religion' which often challenges the priestly approach as we find in the Old Testament and in particular in the writings of the Minor Prophets such as Amos and Micah. In Amos 5, we read that God declares, 'I hate, I despise your feasts and solemn assemblies'. Prophetic religion speaks about social injustice and the judgment of God because it is about what God has done and what God will do.

The third approach to Biblical religion is described as 'wisdom religion'. This, by contrast, is not into church services, nor does it dwell on the acts of God in history. Wisdom religion is about raising children, and dealing with local gossip. It is about coping with a difficult neighbour and about keeping your temper and it is about how one can keep going when under duress. Most importantly, it is about living with a sense of grace and keeping your promises and it is about the perils of making money and the joy of making love. I believe that wisdom religion has more relevance about the practice of modelling our life on the person of Jesus than either the priestly religion or the prophetic.

The 'Age of Belief' that has held sway since the middle of the fourth century can no longer provide us with an authentic model for living, because under this model the message of Jesus became a message about Jesus.

The orthodox Church is more concerned about maintaining a priestly/prophetic religion than a wisdom religion, whereas the day-to-day activity of a faith community is the practice of wisdom religion, which has more practical relevance on a community that is modelling itself on the life of Jesus of Nazareth. This is the importance of wisdom religion as compared to priestly religion and is a new approach for communities of faith. Wisdom religion also requires wisdom spirituality and this in turn develops a wisdom liturgy. Wisdom religion is one that emphasises the seeking of the spirit of sacredness within and between us, and not some external sacred power that we need to invoke to intervene on our behalf.

If we agree that personal relationships are a transforming influence then as companions of the sage Jesus of Nazareth we must use our personal relationship skills to create a more inclusive and caring community. At times, as Jesus has illustrated, to be successful we will need to operate subversively.

It is appropriate to conclude that significant social change can be wrought through the 'Empowering Nature of Friendship'. It doesn't necessarily require a major systemic restructuring to begin. It is within the power of small groups that will effect significant social change.

Many of the greatest movements for change have begun with grassroots face-to-face groups.

The future role of faith communities that embrace the values of their friend Jesus will be in their ability to share and support the development of these personal values with each other. As a community, the role of each individual will include advocating on behalf of people who have been disadvantaged by the dominant values of the wider community. In this way we will be able to ensure that these people will receive the justice and inclusion that they are deserve and are entitled to. This may at times include working with other advocacy groups such as trade unions and social advocacy groups whose values may have developed from an entirely different perspective.

On a wall of the Museum of Methodism in the English city of Bristol, there is a summary of John Wesley's quotes, called *John Wesley's Principles in the Eighteenth Century*, taken from the recorded words of John Wesley. The summary of his beliefs is described as a 'Manifesto'.

1. Reduce the gap between rich people and poor people
2. Help everyone to have a job
3. Help the poorest, including introducing a living wage
4. Offer the best possible education
5. Help everyone to feel they can make a difference
6. Promote tolerance
7. Promote equal treatment of women
8. Create a society based on values and not on profits or and consumerism
9. End all forms of slavery
10. Avoid getting into wars
11. Share the love of God with everyone
12. Care for the environment.

The actual writings of John Wesley which have provided evidence for this manifesto can be found in Appendix C.

How then do we follow the way of Jesus in a world that seems more out of control every day? Further, how do we deal with the wealth gap between the rich and the poor, racism, sexism, immigration, climate change, and a feeling of powerlessness in the face of corruption and misinformation? Faith communities in the future will need to be more concerned with the practical issues of living life harmoniously and justly, rather than a belief in religious doctrines.

Unfortunately, under Constantine, the ethical, social, political movement of Jesus was converted into a religion with all the empirical structures of the Roman Empire. Up until recent times many, as a positive influence in the community have regarded orthodox Christianity worldwide, but recent research has indicated that this is no longer the case.

Today – according to the research into the statistics of Australian society as quoted by my friend and colleague Rev. John Gunson – shows us that regular participation in the life of Christian orthodoxy has been reduced to about 5% of the total population. This finding is supported by the research of Professor Gary Bouma (reported in the *Journal for the Academic Study of Religion*, 30 [2017], pp. 129-43) who also discovered that 52% of teenagers claim no religion but, most importantly, 83% claim that they live ethically without religion.

This evidence supports the belief that most children and in fact a majority of Australians are deeply secularised. It can be concluded that the average Australian has 'written off' the church and religion in general. The hangover of a religious past, which lacked any evidence-based understanding of our world, has no relevance for how to live in the twenty-first century.

When we read the origins of Jesus' teaching from the New Testament, the evidence presents him as a unique, sacred person anointed by God. However, when we examine these writings in the light of recent Biblical scholarship such as that provided by the Jesus Seminar writers such as Marcus Borg, John Dominic Crossan, Bishop John Shelby Spong, Robert Funk and Bernard Brandon Scott to name a few, we discover the historical human Jesus is more a wisdom sage, teacher, healer and advocate for a just and compassionate society than a 'messiah'.

When we examine the ways of Jesus in the light of this information, we discover that he was, at times, a strong opponent of the Jewish religion of his day. Jesus emphasised in his teaching, not the worship of God but the empowering influence of the acceptance of love and respect for each other. For Jesus, the only way to worship was to truly love our neighbour. Hence as John Gunson concludes in his powerful book *God, Ethics and the Secular Society*, 'the teachings of Jesus was not about God or religion but about ethics'.

The information provided by these scholars explains to us that shortly after the death of Jesus the movement that was initiated through his teaching turned him into a 'Messiah' and shaped his adoration into a religious form of Judaism.

As my friend and colleague John Gunson further concludes, 'The movement that Jesus initiated was never intended to be a formalised religion, but a way of life. Jesus' legacy was a social and ethical example of how life should be lived'.

The evidence of recent research into the religious beliefs of Australians as presented by Gary Bouma and Phillip Hughes as well as recent research in the USA, indicates very clearly that the future of faith communities must be established as ethically-based communities, based on a sense of compassion, if their intention is to positively influence everyday living in Australia, and most importantly if they are to address the social problems we are experiencing currently in Australia.

We have witnessed in Australasia over the last two decades a movement of people defining themselves as 'Progressive Christians' who are seeking to contact people of similar interests to explore the relevance of this new scholarship. Many of these group members continue as members of their faith community, but are seeking a deeper understanding of the Jesus message.

In 2012, I conducted a grassroots research of these groups in Australia and New Zealand defined as 'Living the Progressive Dream' and the findings of this study were recorded in the book *Why Weren't We Told*. I concluded that; 'The principal strength of these groups is that they are vibrant discussion groups, exploring contemporary scholarship in a safe, open and inclusive environment'.

These groups were providing an atmosphere where nothing is 'taboo', where hostility and ridicule is not tolerated and where open and frank exchange of ideas is encouraged (pp. 203 ff).

Through this research, we discovered that the majority of the groups we made contact with had been informally established, with no agreed upon structure, and of course, with no formal national or state registration. People who were familiar with the new biblical scholarship surrounding the historical Jesus usually organised these groups, and in most cases there was no defined leader. It was left to a select number of participants in the group to take turns at conducting the meetings.

As Wakeman (2003) writes in relation to her experience in Ireland with similar groups: 'No-one is in charge, no-one is spiritually superior. All are perceived as having gifts to offer'. In most situations, the majority of the group participants were members of the same community of faith, but this did not exclude atheists, agnostics and those from other denominations and faiths. Some groups were aware of similar progressive groups in their state, but as a rule they remained independent and isolated.

In 'Living the Progressive Dream', requests for information were sent out to forty groups asking for a report, in narrative form, of their raison d'être, their programs and their plans for the future, along with any concerns they may harbour. We received twenty-six written responses (a small sample) but the information contained in the responses showed many similarities. Like those in the Taussig study, reported in his book *A New Spiritual Home* (2006), where he discovered that people who joined these groups were seeking open-minded, lively debate on issues of faith. They were also seeking a community that was hospitable and not only tolerant, but accepting of doubts and complex questions which many participants had been wrestling with for years.

These were people who had been struggling with orthodox Christianity and wished to reclaim the message of the historical Jesus as defined by the scholars of the Jesus Seminar. Hal Taussig refers to the people in this emerging movement as 'Progressive Christians', first, because this is the term the people in this new movement use to describe themselves; and secondly, because, they practise their faith with open minds, and open hearts, and are prepared to adjust to change as the term 'progressive' defines.

It is clear that the 'Age of Religion' has been an ineffective response through the belief that it is 'sacred powers' that controlled and ruled the world and religious doctrine and practice was the way to reveal these unseen sacred powers. Orthodoxy has failed and neo-orthodoxy is on the same path if it refuses to ask the moral and ethical questions that impact on all people daily in our society.

If the reasoning presented above is correct, then the structure of our current faith communities must change. How can this occur? In a recent article from *Progressing Spirit* (October 2019), the Rev. Jessica Shine raised this issue in her articles 'Why The Church Must Die'. The information presented in these articles also affirms the findings of Rev. John Gunson's research.

The Rev. Shine from America states: 'The church isn't just dying because in many parts of the USA, it is already dead at least its influence is'. The information presented by the Rev Shine in her articles from 'Progressing Spirituality' supports the research findings in Australia, when she claims that in the USA, the organisation or institution of the church has been elevated in its importance above that of the teachings of the historical Jesus.

The Rev. Shine describes the institution of the church not as Christian orthodoxy but as 'churchianity' because of the prioritising of the Church empire over the message of Jesus. Is it possible that the 'death of the Church' is really the 'good news', because without the death of churchianity, it will be difficult if not impossible to regenerate and reclaim the message of Jesus?

In a similar pattern to that experienced in the Australian scene, there is a world-wide movement where people are describing themselves as 'spiritual but not religious'. It appears that this response is a result of the fact that 'churchianity' does not align with the current secular understanding of social issues such as 'same sex marriage, homosexuality, racism and violence towards women'.

Each time the Christian orthodox church creates a new crusade to justify its relevance, it tends to distance itself from those who are keen to know more about the earthly wisdom of the sagely Jesus.

The claims 'churchianity' has made about Jesus often do not 'stack up' with the research of the scholars from the Jesus Seminar. For example, it was never Jesus' intention to establish an institution in opposition to Judaism because Jesus was more concerned about loving relationships in the way we life our life. For Jesus, the church is not a building or an institution; it is about people and the way they live.

Shine concludes that, as a result of her analysis, 'churchianity must die' because it is a primary tool of the modern supremacist empire, crafted by political powers that want a system that controls rather than connects. Churchianity emphasises that bigger is better and that assets are more important than relationships; whereas the Jesus message is that we need connection with each other with time to listen and to talk with each other to share times together over meals.

These statements by Shine that the church must die for the true message of Jesus to be embraced would not be considered by Jesus to be inappropriate. In John 3:1-9 there is a recorded conversation between Jesus and Nicodemus. When we examine closely this conversation, it appears to support the message of Jessica Shine. In this conversation, Jesus is explaining to Nicodemus that if his life is not being fruitful, then he needs to embrace a life that gives him fulfilment and the only way that this can occur is if he is prepared to let the old life die because only then can a new life and a new soul be reborn. Perhaps this is why Rev. Jessica Shine is explaining that the 'church must die'.

Many people in our community are seeking an apologetic statement from the Christian Church, in particular a statement which apologises for having placed more emphasis on creeds and ancient doctrines (including a literal interpretation of the Bible) rather than the sayings, message and values of the historical Jesus. Many people in the community are aware that the Christian church has oppressed gays and lesbians and in fact all people included in the LGBTQI community. Further, it has treated sex like a disease rather than a divine gift.

As well, in its literal interpretation of the Bible, the Christian church has twisted the words of the Bible to claim that these statements have endorsed slavery, wars, greed, and the rejection of well-researched scientific evidence. And the orthodox Christian church, through its appointing of men to powerful positions, has rejected the equal rights for women. The Rev. Jim Burklo has written his version of how this apology should be phrased (see appendix D).

Therefore the future of the communities of people who call themselves 'friends of historical Jesus' must prioritise the need to share time together over meals and conversations. Jesus honoured and challenged the community that surrounded him because he embraced the value of communing together. The single greatest factor for a meaningful life is meaningful relationships.

Jessica Shine's writings also support the findings of Lisa Jane Miller when she states, 'We are born with an inherent awareness and desire for communion with God yet little of our daily routine fosters this'.

After Jesus' death and resurrection, the spirit of his presence remains with his followers and emphasises that it is the spirit of love and peace which empowers them; and which means they will never again feel alone. The good news is that it is the spirit of love that binds people together and it comes from within.

So if the message of Jesus is to come alive, then, as Shine concludes, the church as we know it must die; and what then can be born and resurrected is a new community based on the spirit of love. Our task is that we must be the midwives of this rebirth.

We must be willing to return to our prophetic calling of living in community with each other and the sacred energy we have been born with, as did Jesus. We must be willing to live as Jesus lived and die as Jesus died, not as a martyr, but as a person opposed to the systems of oppression. As Robin Meyers argues in his book *Spiritual Defiance*, our most important legacy when we die must be, 'a family and friendship network of compassionate loving people'.

The new faith communities could be small groups that gather together in homes, coffee shops and in nature. They will need to gather and share with each other, because they are yearning to connect with each other, and the sacred source of energy that surrounds us. We will share each other's joys and burdens, without the need for an employed minister, priest or pastor or institutional affiliation. Egalitarian communities will be a vision of Jesus and will rise up now in our midst once we move away from the 'Empire' oriented churchianity. Perhaps when churchianity dies, we will then return also to our communal roots as an ecological partner and child of this planet.

How will we structure alternative communal activities of believers in the values of Jesus, which will need to be a structure that will encourage the development of positive, growth-promoting relationships that I have been advocating throughout this book?

My colleague Rev. John Gunson has been recently chairing a committee for the Progressive Christian Network of Victoria to examine alternatives to what Jessica Shine refers to as churchianity. The findings of this committee indicate that the future of the Jesus movement is the way ahead for people seeking a meaningful life but, to achieve success, we need to build the movement from scratch because of the evidence of the failures of churchianity as presented earlier. In his report, the Rev. Gunson has listed a number of important steps to take to ensure the new movement does not fall into the traps of the past.

These steps are that first, the new movement must be ethically based, using the example of the way of Jesus of

Nazareth to become a community of acceptance and love for all people. A community where all people are welcomed, accepted and supported.

A community that encourages all its members to be positively involved in the needs of the wider community, which would include standing in solidarity with those who are seeking justice, freedom and healing.

Leadership of these groups would arise from within by those skilled in leadership. The group size would need to be such where all members are able to participate and take responsibility in the activities.

The members of each individual group would determine how often they would meet and where these meetings would be held. It is quite possible that the groups may wish to share with others their growth and development and to learn from each other and this could occur informally.

The agenda of the group must include the opportunity to relate to and share with all other members on a regular basis, such as sharing in discussion on ethical issues and matters of concern, and the gathering together around meals. Each group could seek from the local community leaders, advice and support on how to be an effective, ethically- and compassionately-based group. Most importantly, the members of the group must be prepared at times to show affection for one another, particularly in times of distress and this requires an ability to be openly honest about one's feelings.

These groups will require members with the personal skills of leadership, communication, organisational and political action skills, as well as the personal social skills of nurturing one another, and particularly by providing an embracing support for new members. This will also require people with the knowledge of the values, ethics, compassion and empathy of the historical Jesus.

A key attribute the group leadership will also require will be the courage and strength to stand in solidarity as did Jesus with people who are disadvantaged, which will at times will require the challenging of authorities, be they political or societal. The members of these new groups must also accept that the spirituality with which they were born is the force that connects them to their world and all other human beings for which they have a responsibility.

Chapter 12
Concluding Comments

IN CONCLUSION, I believe that my research has clearly indicated that the resolving of the worldwide damaging social problems that we are currently facing in Australia, through such issues as violence towards and the rejection of women, including domestic violence, racism and racial vilification through 'hate speech' as well as economic inequality, which cannot be resolved by political systems or the current structure of the orthodox Christian church. The root cause of oppression, violence and domination is primarily due to the lack of compassion. Hence, the way forward is for each and every person to accept responsibility for the way they care for and support each other because it is only when we commit ourselves to the values of care that we can change the world.

I strongly suggest that this can be achieved when we accept the example of the historical Jesus of Nazareth who shows us through his words and actions, that in the world in which we live, there are some things that are more important than fame, money, power and ideology and these are the personal values of compassion, love, and respect that we find in our friendships with others. Jesus embodied a way of life that accepted the realities of existence and pointed to another way, an abundant way, of responding to the reality of life. It was that to be humane we are required to strive together to alleviate human suffering. To be humane is to live the abundant life that Jesus envisaged and this requires us to live by the values Jesus espoused.

Being humane also requires us to affirm the acts of kindness and compassion, whenever and wherever we recognise them, whether it is friends or strangers who commit these acts. Jesus also endorses the act of affirmation, which is the key motivating force that encourages us to act appropriately. I am now at an age that, when I travel on crowded public transport, young people, particularly young Asian students, will stand and offer me a seat. When this occurs, I thank them and most times I tell them that their parents would be proud of them.

Each time this happens, I receive words of appreciation and usually a beautiful smile.

Affirmation can bring us joy and a sense of importance and in turn the encouragement to continue acting with love and compassion. Not only does it impact on the person showing kindness, but it also impacts on those who overhear the conversation of appreciation for the kindness that is shown. These acts of compassion and kindness come from the creative spirit that is within all of us, and that we name as God.

The Rev. Dr Francis Macnabs' interpretation of Psalm 67 in his book *A Fine Wind is Blowing* emphasises the importance of affirmation when he writes, 'We ordinary human beings search for that assurance and that confirmation that we are fully accepted and fully blessed. May the Eternal Presence be like a light shining gently on our faces? If only the whole world could know that acceptance. If only every nation, every race, every person, could feel the positive influence of that Eternal Presence. Everyone would sing their common song of peace, exhilaration and joy. Let the good harvests of the earth be shared with generosity and justice. Let people from all walks of life come to their full awareness that they are part of one family on earth. May they come together in common purpose? May people from every part and place of the earth sing together, and know they are part of a new humanity by the blessing of the Eternal Presence'.

So if we have been asked the question, 'Is our God dead?' as Nietzsche suggests, we can respond by saying that the God we believe in is alive, and within us, and the evidence of this is how we show compassion and care for each other. So if our God is alive and present in our lives, how then should we respond to the world around us?

Over the years, a number of people have raised with me their concern that the church is too political, especially the Uniting Church. I have also been told by a number of people that I am too political in my comments including those that I make from the pulpit. I am not the only preacher who has had this accusation levelled at them over the years and the incidence of these occurrences of challenges seem to increase during an election time.

A number of my ministerial colleagues also testify that often the criticism of being too political comes from people who disagree with the statements being made. It appears sometimes that a point is political or not political depending on whether there is agreement or no agreement.

I am also very much aware that people take their political allegiances seriously and do not take kindly to their preferences being questioned or lampooned. I recently received, by email, a liberal political announcement regarding criticisms of union representatives and for a piece of sheer devilment I sent an email back lampooning the message. To my surprise, I received a number of emails in return, casting doubts on the legitimacy of my birth and questioning my views in language that would make a sailor blush. My mental state was also questioned. All of which indicates how seriously people take their politics.

My mother never believed in the old adage you must never talk politics or religion in our house, as we loved discussions on both because we often saw them as being integrated. However, I must admit that we were sceptical of both and so most of our family discussions were spiced with lots of humour. As an adult, I remember answering a knock on the door one weekend to be confronted by a young salesman who opened his conversation by saying that he wasn't there to talk politics or religion, at which point I told him to get lost because I liked both.

However, I must say at this point that if my irreverence of both religion and politics has caused people concern and upset, then I am sorry. If people have considered me to be too political from a party political perspective, then I again apologise. My intention has always been to stimulate discussion and challenge assumptions.

But there is a more serious issue being raised here and it revolves around the question: what is politics and should it be kept out of religion? One theologian once remarked that mixing politics and religion is like asking an octopus to play the bagpipes; in the end, the bagpipes play the octopus. The religious conservative groups in the USA have become a powerful political lobby group. These groups claim much of the credit for the election of past presidents such as George W. Bush.

However, for those people old enough to remember 50 or 60 years ago here in Australia, there was the rise of the 'industrial workers groups' initiated by B. A Santamaria, a very close friend of the Catholic Archbishop Mannix. In the 1940s and 50s, these groups were strongly backed by the Catholic Church and in particular the Archbishop. The groups were established primarily to weaken the power of the trade unions, because the Catholic Church considered that the unions were a breeding ground for Communism. It is an issue that still creates a sour taste in the mouths of old Labor Party stalwarts.

The Catholic Church at this time was instructing its members through its priests to vote for the Democratic Labour Party, many believed that this action kept the Liberals in power through the fifties and sixties. So religion has, through history, been involved in politics and in some cases the manipulation of political events.

In recent times, we have had Cardinal Pell enter the debate about 'Global Warming' and the Rev. Tim Costello encouraging people on at least two occasions to vote Labor at the 2007 election. His aim, of course, was to ensure we gave more money for overseas aid and that we also signed the Kyoto agreement.

Is this being political? What does it mean to be political? And should Church leaders be so blatantly party political? Politics is defined as the theory and practice of government. Are we political when we support or disagree with the theory and practice of government? Is there any time when as individual Christians or as the Church body we can challenge the theory and practice of government? For example was Nelson Mandela correct in challenging the apartheid government of South Africa? When Martin Luther King challenged the government of the United States of America for its racist policies, was he being political. Or when Dietrich Bonhoeffer in the 1930s not only opposed the government of Germany of his time but actively participated in trying to bring it to an end through the assassination of the political leader Adolf Hitler. Was he wrong in doing so? Where did his actions sit with his Christian beliefs?

When we read the parables of Jesus and the Old Testament Prophets, we can see that they were actively involved in questioning the power elites of the day, which included religious as well as government officials. I urge all to read the book of the prophet Amos as an example, particularly Amos 5:11-15. In verse 5:15 we read, 'Hate evil and love good, and establish justice in the gate'. Amos is clearly telling us that justice for all is our responsibility if we believe in a loving God.

Hence, if we see injustice for one group be they refugees, be they Muslims, be they the poor or sick, be they disabled or our indigenous brothers and sisters, and we say nothing,

Concluding Comments

is the Church or are we as Christians complicit in supporting their disempowerment? At this point, I am reminded of the well-known saying: 'Evil occurs when good people do nothing'.

In operation 'Sovereign Borders', will the armed services personnel who carry out the instructions of the government be personally liable for prosecution if a person dies from their actions?

Clearly, Orthodoxy has failed and neo-orthodoxy is on the same path if it refuses to ask the moral and ethical questions that affect all people in the twenty-first century. More than this, the future of 'faith communities' will be determined by their actions, based on their ethics. They will be regarded not for what they say but for what they do and how they live and how they defend the rights of others.

I continue to be interested in and enjoy the company of people. As well I seek to develop personal and enduring relationships. I am very enthusiastic about the joy of life and want to share my understanding of the presence of the divine with others. At times, there will be a need to express my own understanding of the truth, but this must be done with sensitivity to the needs of others.

Nurturing the strengths and encouraging the development of mutually beneficial relationships with all members will best serve a congregation/community of faith. Only then can we stand in solidarity with other human beings and share our journey with those outside the community. I believe this is possible if we actively follow the way of Jesus of Nazareth who has revealed in his words and actions the reality of the sacred.

It is appropriate to conclude that significant social change can be wrought through the 'Empowering Nature of Friendship'. It is also important to realise that this doesn't necessarily require a major systemic restructuring to begin with because it is within the power of small groups to effect significant social change.

History reveals that many of the greatest movements for change have begun with grassroots face-to-face groups. If we agree that personal relationships are a transforming influence, then as companions of the sage Jesus of Nazareth we must use our personal relationship skills to create a more inclusive and caring community. It is also important to accept that to be successful there will be times when we need to operate subversively. This may also require us to express a spiritual defiance with force, when it comes to challenging the current practice of Christian orthodoxy along with politically determined injustice against those in need.

There is some evidence that orthodox Christianity or, as the Rev. Shine suggests, 'churchianity', is dying and in many situations is already dead. This book is aimed at raising an awareness of what I describe as 'secular spirituality', which is the recognition that a sacred energy is present in our everyday lives, which we must reclaim as the message of the historical Jesus, when he states, that the sacred energy we call God is within us and between us and comes to visibility in the way we demonstrate our love for each other. Hence, the death of the church as we know it is not the death of the Spiritual energy source we call God. So we need to celebrate this message by reaching out with compassion to others,

Concluding Comments

because if we don't many people will continue to suffer as has been expressed earlier in the book. The term 'secular spirituality' affirms that every person regardless of church affiliation has access to a sacred energy, and it is this sacred energy that connects him or her to other humans and the living world that surrounds us from the time of our birth.

However, by raising this issue, I am aware that it will cause deep concern for some members of orthodox Christian communities. Many of these believers will not only be concerned, but they will be naturally offended by these conclusions, and this being the case we must listen carefully to their concerns.

There will be others, who have been struggling with accepting the programs, policies and statements of belief long proposed by Christian orthodoxy, and these people may even more so embrace the possibility of the sacred spirit alive within each of us, which is revealed in life, words, and actions of Jesus of Nazareth.

I sincerely hope that this book raises for all people the belief that the message of Jesus is as relevant today as it was 2000 years ago and if embraced will bring to our world the much needed sense of our responsibilities for the loving care, support and advocacy of those in need. For this to be successful we will need to embrace the boldness of the Spirit of life which will transform us, together with the compassionate nature of Jesus which will be our inspiration, because by embracing the ethics of Jesus we will transform the world to be a centre for love and justice.

As mentioned earlier, the Jews have a term called 'Tikkun Olam' which is a concept defined by 'acts of kindness performed to heal, repair and transform the world'. The term is often used when discussing issues of social policy, ensuring there is a safeguard to those who may be disadvantaged.

I firmly believe that the future of those communities who are committed to the ethical values and way of life of the historical compassionate Jesus, will be a focal point for the renewing of our world, because the evidence as presented here is clear, that the world of today is in desperate need of repair and transformation through acts of kindness.

Bibliography

Ainsworth, MDS, Blehar, MC, Waters E, Wall, S. *Patterns of Attachment: A Psychological Study of the Strange Situation*. Lawrence Erlbaum Associates Publications New Jersey, 1978.

Armstrong Karen. *Twelve Steps to a Compassionate Life*. The Bodley Head London, 2011.

Bessler-Northcutt Joe. 'Learning to See God' in Jesus Seminar, Dewey Arthur et al. *The Historical Jesus Goes to Church*. Polebridge Press California. 2004.

Bessler-Northcutt 'Facing Up to Hard Questions: Christian Faith' in Miller Robert J. *The Future of the Christian Tradition*. Polebridge Press Santa Rosa California. 2007.

Bonhoeffer Dietrich. *The Cost of Discipleship*. SCM Press Ltd. 1959.

Borg Marcus. *The Heart of Christianity*. HarperSanFrancisco. 2003

_____ *Meeting Jesus Again for the First Time*. HarperSanFrancisco. 1995.

Bodycomb John. *Two Elephants in the Room*. Spectrum Publications Pty Ltd. Richmond Victoria. 2018.

Bouma, Gary and Annan, Halafoff, 'Australia's changing religious profile – rising nones and Pentecostals, declining Protestants in superdiversity: Views from the 2016 Census'. *Journal for the Academic Study of Religion* 30 (2017) 129-143.

Bowlby John. *The Making and Breaking of Affectional Bonds*. Travistock Publications, London. 1979.

Burnside Julian. *Watching Brief Reflections on Human Rights, Law, and Justice*. Scribe Publications Pty Ltd. Melbourne

Cranmer John & Grierson Denham. *Walking on Bare Bones*. Morning Star Publishing, Melbourne. 2017.

Crossan John Dominic. *The Historical Jesus*. HarperSanFrancisco. 1992.

_____ *Jesus A Revolutionary Biography*. HarperSanFrancisco. 1995.

_____ *The Birth of Christianity*. HarperSanFrancisco. 1998.

Finlan Stephen. *Problems with Atonement*. Liturgical Press Minnesota. 2005.

Fox Matthew. *Original Blessing*. Bear & Company Santa Fe. 1983.

_____ *Creation Spirituality*. HarperSanFrancisco. 1991.

Funk Robert, Roy Hoover and the Jesus Seminar. *The Five Gospels: What Did Jesus Really Say?*. HarperSanFrancisco. 1993.

_____ *The Acts of Jesus: What Did Jesus Really Do?*. HarperSanFrancisco. 1998. Copyright by Polebridge Press.

Galston David. *Embracing the Human Jesus A Wisdom Path for Progressive Christianity*. Polebridge Press. 2012.

Geraghty Chris. *Jesus the forgotten feminist*. Garratt Publishing Melbourne. 2018.

Gunson John. *God, Ethics and the Secular Society*. Morning Star Publishing Melbourne. 2016.

Habel Norman. *A Bloke Called Jesus*. Rigby Publishers Adelaide. 1982.

Holiday Ryan. *Ego is the Enemy*. Profile Books London. 2017.

Hunt Rex A. E, & Jenks Gregory C. eds. *Wisdom and Imagination*. Morning Star Publishing Melbourne. 2016.

Hunt Rex A E. & John W. H. Smith eds. *Why Weren't We Told? A Handbook on Progressive Christianity.* Polebridge Press. 2013.

Huntley Rebecca. 'Australia Fair' *Quarterly Essay.* McPhersons Printing Group. 2019.

Hyde Dudley. *Rescuing Jesus: A Heretic Handbook.* Mandarin Publishing Australia. 1997.

Mackay Hugh. *Why Don't People Listen.* Pan Macmillan. 1949.

_____ *The Good Life, What makes Life Worth living.* Pan Macmillan Australia. 2016.

_____ *Australia Reimagined. Towards a more compassionate, less anxious society.* Pan Macmillan. 2018.

Macnab Francis. *A Fine Wind is Blowing.* Spectrum Publications, Richmond Victoria. 2006.

McKnight Scott. *The Jesus Creed Loving God Loving Others.* Paraclete Press. 2004.

Meyers Robin. *The Underground Church: Reclaiming the Subversive Way of Jesus.* Jossey-Bass A Wiley Imprint. 2012.

_____ *Spiritual Defiance: Building a Beloved Community of Resistance.* Yale University Press New Haven. 2015.

Miller Lisa. *The Spiritual Child.* Picador New York. 2015.

Bibliography

Morwood Michael. *Prayers For Progressive Christians.* Kelmore Publications. 2018.

Nolan Albert. *Jesus Before Christianity.* Orbis Books New York. 1978

Nouwen Henri. *Reaching Out.* Image Books Doubleday New York. 1975.

O'Murchu Diarmuid. *Adult Faith growing in Wisdom and Understanding.* Orbis Books New York. 2010.

_____ *Incarnation A New Evolutionary Threshold.* Orbis Books New York. 2017.

_____ *Inclusivity A Gospel Mandate.* Orbis Books. 2015.

_____ *Christianity's Dangerous Memory.* Crossroad. 2011.

Patterson Stephen. *The God of Jesus: the historical Jesus and the search for meaning.* Trinity Press International Pennsylvania. 1998.

Robinson John A. T. *New Reformation?* SCM Canterbury Press. 1965.

_____ *Honest To God.* SCM Press. 1962.

Rogers Carl. *On Becoming a Person.* Constable London. 1967

Shine, Jessica. 'Why the Church must die – Part !' Progressing Spirit https://progressingspirit.com/2019/10/24/why-the-church-must-die-part-1/

Smith John W. H. & Hunt Rex A. E. Eds. *New Life Rediscovering Faith*. Morning Star Publications Melbourne. 2013.

Smith John W. H. *Honest To Good*. Morning Star Publications Melbourne Australia. 2016.

Spong, John Shelby, *Unbelievable: Why Neither Ancient Creeds Nor the Reformation Can Produce a Living Faith Today*. Harper One USA. 2018.

Squire Anne. 'Radical Inclusion,' in *The Emerging Christian Way*, Borg Marcus et al. pp. 143ff.

Taussig Hal ed. *A New New Testament*. Houghton Mifflin Harcourt Boston. 2013.

———— *A New Spiritual Home*. Polebridge Press. 2006.

Wakeman Hilary. *Saving Christianity: New Thinking for Old Beliefs*. The Liffey Press. 2013.

Wink Walter. *Jesus and Nonviolence: A Third Way*. Fortress Press Minneapolis USA. 2003.

———— *The Human Being: Jesus and the Enigma of the Son of Man*. Fortress Press Minneapolis. 2002

Appendix A

Uluru Statement From The Heart

We, gathered at the 2017 National Constitutional Convention, coming from all points of the southern sky, make this statement from the heart:

Our Aboriginal and Torres Strait Islander tribes were the first sovereign Nations of the Australian continent and its adjacent islands, and possessed it under our own laws and customs. This our ancestors did, according to the reckoning of our culture, from the Creation, according to the common law from 'time immemorial', and according to science more than 60,000 years ago.

This sovereignty is a spiritual notion: the ancestral tie between the land, or 'mother nature', and the Aboriginal and Torres Strait Islander peoples who were born there from, remain attached thereto, and must one day return thither to be united with our ancestors. This link is the basis of the ownership of the soil, or better, of sovereignty. It has never been ceded or extinguished, and co-exists with the sovereignty of the Crown.

How could it be otherwise? That peoples possessed a land for sixty millennia and this sacred link disappears from world history in merely the last two hundred years?

With substantive constitutional change and structural reform, we believe this ancient sovereignty can shine through as a fuller expression of Australia's nationhood.

Proportionally, we are the most incarcerated people on the planet. We are not an innately criminal people. Our children are aliened from their families at unprecedented rates. This cannot be because we have no love for them. And our youth languish in detention in obscene numbers. They should be our hope for the future.

These dimensions of our crisis tell plainly the structural nature of our problem. This is the torment of our powerlessness.

We seek constitutional reforms to empower our people and take a rightful place in our own country. When we have power over our destiny our children will flourish. They will walk in two worlds and their culture will be a gift to their country.

We call for the establishment of a First Nations Voice enshrined in the Constitution.

Makarrata is the culmination of our agenda: the coming together after a struggle. It captures our aspirations for a fair and truthful relationship with the people of Australia and a better future for our children based on justice and self-determination.

We seek a Makarrata Commission to supervise a process of agreement-making between governments and First Nations and truth-telling about our history.

Uluru Statement From The Heart

In 1967 we were counted, in 2017 we seek to be heard. We leave base camp and start our trek across this vast country. We invite you to walk with us in a movement of the Australian people for a better future.

Appendix B
Common Dreams Statement 2019

We the participants in the Common Dreams Conference, from diverse places and faith traditions, in 2019 hereby

- accept and celebrate the Uluru Statement from the Heart
- recognise the sovereignty of the Aboriginal peoples as enunciated in the accompanying Uluru Statement from the Heart
- acknowledge their rich creation spirituality that continues to make a vital contribution to the diverse culture of Australia and

We call upon Federal, State and Local Governments and all people of Australia to drastic action

- to call for constitutional change to embrace this sovereignty
- to exercise restorative justice (Makarrata) in its full extent as defined by Aboriginal Peoples
- to enshrine a First Nations Voice in the Constitution via the treaty process

and

Common Dreams Statement 2019

We challenge and call all faith communities of Australia to action

- to endorse the Common Dreams Statement
- to urge the governments of Australia to accept and implement the Uluru Statement from the Heart
- to activate the Treaty process so that there is ongoing justice for the First Peoples of Australia on the basis that the shared Abrahamic traditions embrace the Creation Spirituality of the Scriptures, but especially in the Genesis account of Abraham, who
- became an ally and friend of the indigenous custodians of Canaan
- recognised and swore by the Creator Spirit of Canaan (El Elyon)
- formed a treaty with a Canaanite community, a treaty that embraced the land.

This statement recognises the collusion of governments and churches in the dispossession and cultural and physical genocide of Aboriginal and Torres Strait Islander Peoples.

The Common Dreams Conference is a conference of progressive Christians and this statement is the result of their deliberations led by Professor Emeritus Norman Habel in July 2019.

Appendix C

The Words of Rev John Wesley in the Eighteenth Century

1. Be ye ready to distribute to everyone, according to their necessity.
2. Wickedly, devilishly false is that common objection, 'They are poor only because they are idle... Find work them work... They will then earn and eat their own bread'.
3. How many are there in this Christian country that toil, labour, sweat... but struggle with weariness and hunger together? Is it not worse for one, after a hard days labour, to come back to a poor, cold, dirty, uncomfortable lodging, and to find there not even the food which is needful to repair his wasted strength?
4. Beware of that common but, accursed, way of making children a parrot... Regard not how much, but how well, to what good purpose, they read... The end of education... is to help us to discover every false judgment

of our minds, and to subdue every wrong passion in our hearts... and to understand as much as we are able.
5. I continue to dream... of the time when the potential of each person can be unleashed
6. Though we cannot think alike, may we not love alike? May we not be of one heart, though we are not of one opinion.
7. May not women as well as men bear an honourable part... yield not to the vile bondage any longer. You, as well as men, are rational creatures.
8. In seeking happiness from riches, you are only striving to drink out of empty cups. And let them be painted and gilded ever so finely, they are empty still.
9. Let none serve you but by his own act and deed, by his own voluntary action. Away with all whips, all chains all compulsion!... Do with everyone else as you would he should do to you.
10. War: What farther proof of do we need of the utter degeneracy of all nations from the plainest principles of reason and virtue? Of the absolute want, both of common sense and common humanity, which runs through the whole race of mankind?
11. I look upon the world as my parish, thus far I mean, that within whatever part of it I am, I judge it... my bounden duty is to declare unto all that are willing to hear the glad tidings of salvation.
12. Lead us beyond an exclusive concern for the well-being of other human beings to the broader concern for the well-being of the birds in our backyards, the fish in our rivers, and every living creature on the face of the earth.

www.ingramcontent.com/pod-product-compliance
Lightning Source LLC
Chambersburg PA
CBHW010706020526
44107CB00082B/2684